I0423357

Disclaimer

The information in this eBook reflects the opinions of the author and is not intended to replace medical or psychological advice, or any other professional advice. This EBook is not intended to diagnose or treat any psychological or medical conditions or disorders. If you are in need psychological or medical treatment, consult with a certified and licensed professional before determining whether the information in this book should be used.

© Dec' 2015 Mumbai

Know India – Culture, Places and Much More

Table Of Contents

Introduction

India is a vast country, with diverse cultures and ancient civilization. There are a number of religious groups residing in India. In India we find the oldest pilgrimage tradition in the whole world. The practice of pilgrimage in India is so deeply embedded in the cultural psyche and the number of pilgrimage sites is so large that the entire subcontinent may actually be regarded as one grand and continuous sacred place. The earliest sources of information on the matter of sacred space come from the Rig Veda and the Atharva Veda.

Following the Vedic period the practice of pilgrimage seems to have become quite common, as is evident from sections of the great epic, the Mahabharata (350 BC), which mentions more than 300 sacred sites spanning the sub-continent. By the time of the Puranas, the number of sacred sites had grown considerably, reflecting both the ongoing assimilation of aboriginal sacred places and the increased importance of pilgrimage as a customary religious practice.

Hindus call the sacred places tirthas and the action of going on a pilgrimage is called tirtha-yatra. The word tirtha means river ford, steps to a river, or place of pilgrimage. In Vedic times the word may have concerned only those sacred places associated with water, but by the time of the Mahabharata, tirtha had come to denote any holy place, be it a lake, mountain, forest, or cave. Tirthas are more than physical locations, however. Pious Hindus believe them to be spiritual fords, the meeting place of heaven and earth, the locations where one crosses the endless cycle of birth, death and rebirth to reach the shore of liberation.

Ajmer Sharif

The Lake city of Ajmer is well known for the Dargah of Sufi saint Khwaja Moin-ud-din Chishti. The 'Dargah Sharif' in Ajmer is held in great esteem by devotees of all communities.

Bodh Gaya

The founder of Buddhism, Gautama Buddha, attained enlightenment under the sacred Bodhi tree at Bodhgaya. Bodhgaya is one of the four most sacred pilgrimage places for the Buddhists.

Char Dham

Char Dham (sacred Hindu shrines of Badrinath, Kedarnath, Gangotri and Yamunotri) are situated in the snow-covered reaches of the lofty Garhwal Himalayas, Uttaranchal.

Golden Temple

The Golden Temple or "Darbar Sahib" at Amritsar is the most sacred place for the Sikhs. The Golden temple symbolizes the magnificence of the Sikhs all over the world.

Haridwar

Haridwar is one of the most important Hindu pilgrim places of India. Haridwar has very rich religious and cultural heritage. In the Hindu scriptures, Haridwar is known by the name of Mayapur.

Jain Pilgrimage

India is the land where Jainism originated. Today, around 3.2 million Jain devotees live in India. Across the length and breadth of India lay the Jain temples and shrines and hold immense attraction

Mansarovar

Mount Kailash is a sacred pilgrimage place of Asia and lies in the South-West of Tibetan autonomous region of China-Nagri, towering 6714 meters (22022 ft) above the Tibetan Plateau.

Mathura

Mathura is an important place of Hindu pilgrimage. Mathura is also known as the Brajbhoomi - the land where Lord Krishna was born and spent his youth. Mathura is located on the banks of River Yamuna.

Nashik

Nashik is famous as one of the important pilgrimage centers of India. According to mythology Rama, the king of Ayodhya, made Nashik his temporary residence during the 14 years of his exile.

Prayag

Prayag, where river Ganga and Yamuna meet, is one of the ancient pilgrimage centers of India. Prayag is situated in Allahabad. Prayag is venerated in the hymns of the Rig Veda.

Puri

Puri is one of the ancient pilgrimage centers of India. Puri is located on the Orissa coast, 60 km from Bhubaneswar. Puri is among the four sacred "Dhams" (Puri, Dwarka, Rameswaram and Badrinath) of the Hindus.

Rameshwaram

Rameshwaram is situated at the tip of the Indian peninsula. In the Hindu mythology Rameshwaram is considered a sacred place for the Hindus. Legends have it that Lord Rama built a bridge across the sea

Ujjain

Ujjain is one of the oldest cities of India. It is located in the Malwa region of Madhya Pradesh state. In ancient times Ujjain was known by the names of Ujjayini and Avanti. It is situated on the eastern bank of River Shipra.

Varanasi

Varanasi is the oldest and the most sacred place for the Hindus. Varanasi, also known as the holy city, combines in itself the cultural essence and mysticism of India. Varanasi stands on the banks of river Ganga

Badrinath

Badrinath Temple is located in the state of Uttranchal in India. Nestled between the twin mountains of "Nar" and "Narayan", the holy Badrinath pilgrimage is visited by scores of devotees every year.

Belur Math

Belur was the ancient capital city of the Hoysala Empire. Belur math is a major tourist destination in Karnataka. The exact location of Belur Math is in the Hassan district of Karnataka.

Dwarka

The holy Dwarka temple is located in the state of Gujarat located on the West of India. It is an important pilgrimage for all Hindus and is considered to be the ancient kingdom of Lord Krishna.

Guruvayoor Temple

The Guruvayoor Temple is one of the most visited temples in South India. Located in Thrissur (Trichur) district of Kerala in India, this temple is dedicated to Lord Krishna, an incarnation of Lord Vishnu of the Hindu trinity.

Patna Sahib

The capital city of Patna is regarded as very sacred by the Sikhs in India. The tenth Guru of the Sikhs, Guru Gobind Singh was born here. The Patna Sahib Gurudwara is considered to be one of the holiest of the five

Pushkar

Located in the state of Rajasthan in India, Pushkar pilgrimage site is one of the holiest in India. This small town has around 500 temples and is considered to be very sacred by the Hindus.

Puttaparthi

Puttaparthi is a small dusty village located in Anantapur district in the state of Andhra Pradesh in India. It has now attained international as well as national fame because of the glory of Bhagvan Shri Sathya Sai Baba.

Rajgir

Rajgir was the ancient capital city of the kings of Magadha. The name Rajgir literally means "House of the King". Rajgir pilgrimage is a very important Buddhist site since Lord Buddha spent 12 years over here

Ranakpur Temple

Ranakpur is a small village in the state of Rajasthan in India. An otherwise ordinary village to look at, the place is famous for its Ranakpur Temple, which has some splendid carvings and architecture.

Shirdi

There is nothing dandy or gaudy about Shirdi Sai Temple. The small temple is located in a sleepy little town called Shirdi in the state of Maharashtra in India. Don't expect to see commercialization

Siddhivinayak Temple

Regarded as one of the most popular and religious temples in India, Siddhivinayak Temple located in Prabhadevi, Mumbai, is visited by devout believers from all walks of life.

Somnath Temple

Located in the state of Gujarat in India, the famous Somnath Temple is a very sacred Hindu pilgrimage site. It is dedicated to Lord Shiva and is considered to be one of the twelve "Jyotirlingas" (lighted lingas)

Tirupati Balaji

Located in a small district called Chittoor in southern Andhra Pradesh, is the famous Tirupati Balaji Temple of India. This temple is supposed to be the richest temple in India.

Vaishali

A small village in the state of Bihar, Vaishali is a very famous Buddhist pilgrimage in India. The name "Vaishali" means prosperity and the place seems to live upto its name.

Vaishno Devi

Located in the mighty Trikuta Mountains at a distance of 60 kilometers from Jammu, is the famous Vaishno Devi Temple. One of the most visited and worshipped pilgrimages in India.

IntroDuction

India is a vast country, peopled with diverse and ancient civilizations, and its religious geography is highly complex. To grasp the complexity of the situation, it is important to consider two aspects of Indian life: its characteristic of being an ethnic and cultural mosaic, and the ancient rural foundations of many of its religious and cultural patterns.

The process of racial and cultural mixture that began in India 5000-10,000 years ago has been continuous into historical times. Although isolated from the rest of Asia by oceans on three sides and impassable mountain ranges to the north, India has experienced a near-constant influx of differing cultural influences, coming by way of the northwest and the southeast (including extremely ancient migrations from the drowned continent of Sundaland, which had been in the general region of contemporary Indonesia). India in the third millennium BC was inhabited in the tropical south by a people called the Dravidians, in the central and northeastern regions by aboriginal hill and forest tribes, and in the northwest by the highly advanced Indus Valley civilization known as the Harappan culture.

The religion of the city-building Harappan peoples seems to have been a fertility cult centered on the Great Mother, while the rural Dravidians and the various tribal cultures worshipped a wide variety of nature spirits, both benevolent and demonic. Anthropological theories of the 1800's and 1900's (deriving from a biased Eurocentric outlook) stated that around 1800 BC a nomadic people, called the Aryans, entered northwest India from the steppes of Central Asia. A large amount of archaeological, scriptural, linguistic and mythological research conducted during the past few decades has now shown this earlier theory to be inaccurate. While it is certainly true that migrations of different cultural groups did enter India from the northwest during ancient times, it is now abundantly clear that a highly sophisticated culture had already been thriving in the Indus valley region long before the supposed entrance of the hypothetical invaders from Central Asia.

What these archaic people already living in northwest India called themselves we do not know, but the term 'Aryans' is no longer considered suitable for them. Current scholarship has accepted the term 'Harappan' following the naming of one that culture's great cities as Harappa in the early 1900's. Scholars have also significantly pushed back the date of the Harappan culture to approximately 3000 BC (or earlier), rendering it simultaneous with the oldest cultures of Egypt and Mesopotamia. The Harappan culture possessed a sophisticated religion called Vedism (again, we do not know what the people themselves called their religion), which worshipped powerful gods such as Indra, the god of rain; Agni, the god of fire; and Surya, the sun god. During the millennia of the Harappan culture the religion of Vedism developed an increasingly complex form with esoteric rituals and magical chants, and these were later codified in the sacred Hindu texts known as the Vedas.

The religion identified as Hinduism did not actually appear until the centuries preceding the Christian era. Hinduism is an aggregation of the religious beliefs and practices deriving from the Vedism and fertility cults of the Harappan peoples, and the animistic, shamanistic, and devotional practices of the widely varying, rural-dwelling indigenous cultures of south, central, and eastern India. Adding to and further enriching this mix were the concurrently developing religions of Jainism and Buddhism. Indian culture has thus developed a fascinating collection of religious beliefs and customs that range from simple animistic worship of nature spirits in a common rock or tree to the complex, highly codified Brahmanic rituals practiced at the great pilgrimage centers.

In India we find the oldest continually operating pilgrimage tradition in the entire world. The practice of pilgrimage in India is so deeply embedded in the cultural psyche and the number of pilgrimage sites is so large that the entire subcontinent may actually be regarded as one grand and continuous sacred space. Our earliest sources of information on the matter of sacred space come from the Rig Veda and the Atharva Veda. While the act of pilgrimage is not specifically discussed in these texts, mountain valleys and the confluences of rivers are spoken of with reverence, and the merits of travel to such places are mentioned. Following the Vedic period the practice of pilgrimage seems to have become quite common, as is evident from sections of the great epic, the Mahabharata (350 BC), which mentions more than 300 sacred sites spanning the sub-continent. It is probable that most of these sites had long been considered sacred by the aboriginal inhabitants of the region and only later came to be listed in the Mahabharata as different regions came under the influence of Hinduism. By the time of the writing of the Puranas (sacred texts of the 2nd to 15th centuries AD), the number of sacred sites listed had grown considerably, reflecting both the ongoing assimilation of aboriginal sacred places and the increased importance of pilgrimage as a customary religious practice.

Hindus call the sacred places to which they travel tirthas, and the action of going on a pilgrimage tirtha-yatra. The Sanskrit word tirtha means river ford, steps to a river, or place of pilgrimage. In Vedic times the word may have concerned only those sacred places associated with water, but by the time of the Mahabharata, tirtha had come to denote any holy place, be it a lake, mountain, forest, or cave. Tirthas are more than physical locations, however. Devout Hindus believe them to be spiritual fords, the meeting place of heaven and earth, the locations where one crosses over the river of samsara (the endless cycle of birth, death and rebirth) to reach the distant shore of liberation. Writing in Banaras: City of Light, Diana Eck speaks of tirthas as being

...primarily associated with the great acts and appearances of the gods and heroes of Indian myth and legend. As a threshold between heaven and earth, the tirtha is not only a place for the upward crossings of people's prayers and rites, it is also a place for the downward crossings of the gods. These divine descents are the well-known avataras of the Hindu tradition. Indeed, the words tirtha and avatara come from related verbal roots....one might say that the avataras descend, opening the doors of the tirthas so that men and women may ascend in their rites and prayers.

Although tirthas are primarily those places where a god or goddess or some spirit has dwelled or is still dwelling, there is another reason certain places may be accorded sanctity in the Hindu tradition. Saintly individuals who lead exemplary lives imbue their environments with the holiness that accrues from their spiritual practices. Devotees who had visited the saints while they were alive often continued to seek inspiration in the same places after the saint had died. Over many centuries, folk tales about the lives of the saints attained legendary proportions, attracting pilgrims from great distances. If miracles were reported at the shrine, the saint's legends would spread across the entire country, attracting still more pilgrims.

In India all temples are considered sacred places and thus religious visitors to the temples may be described as pilgrims. For the purpose of our discussion, however, for a temple to be considered a true pilgrimage shrine it must have a long-term history of attracting pilgrims from a geographic area beyond its immediate region. Given this condition, the number of pilgrimage sites in India is still extremely large; one text, the Kalyana Tirthanka, describes 1,820 shrines of importance.

Based on years of research and pilgrimage in India, I have chosen a smaller number of shrines, approximately 150, as the primary pilgrimage sites. Those sites include the Four Dhams or Divine Abodes at the four compass points; the Seven Sacred Cities and their primary temples; the Jyotir, Svayambhu, and Pancha Bhutha Linga temples; the Shakti Pitha temples; the Kumbha Mela sites; major Vaishnava sites; the Nava Graha Sthalas (temples of the planets); the seven sacred rivers (Ganga, Yamuna, Saraswati, Godavari, Narmada, Kaveri, and the Sarayu); the four Mutts of Sri Adi Sankaracharya (Badrinath/Joshimath, Puri, Sringeri, and Dwarka); the Arupadaividu (the six sacred places of Lord Kumara); and certain other shrines that do not fit into any of the categories listed here.

In discussing pilgrimage places in the Hindu tradition, it is important to say a few words about the number and diversity of deities in Hinduism and about the iconic and aniconic forms in which those deities are found. The personification of the mysterious forces of the universe into the anthropomorphic deities of the Hindu tradition involves both a convergence into certain supreme deities (the main three deities today are the gods Shiva and Vishnu and the goddess Shakti) and a splintering into a myriad of lesser deities. Certain writers call this polytheism, but the term is inaccurate in this case. No Hindu seriously believes in the multiplicity of gods but rather is aware that each of the many gods and goddesses are merely aspects of the One God (who is also the god of all other religions). The majority of Hindus ally their beliefs with one or the other of the three cults, worshipping Shiva, Vishnu, or Shakti as the highest principle. In doing so they do not deny the existence of the other two deities but regard them as complementary, though minor, expressions of the same divine power. Hinduism is thus, in its essence, monotheistic; a Hindu's worship of a particular personal deity is always done with the awareness that all deities are simply representations of one unconditioned, transcendental, supreme existence, known as Brahman. Each of the greater and lesser deities is understood as a sort of window or lens through which the whole of reality may be glimpsed.

The primary intention of a pilgrim's visit to a holy site is to receive the darshan of the deity resident in the temple's inner sanctum or open-air shrine. The word darshan, difficult to translate into English, generally means the pilgrim having a sight and/or experience of the deity. Hindus believe that the deity is actually manifest in the image, statue, or icon of the temple. To receive the darshan of the deity is to have a spiritual communion with it. The image of the deity may either be an iconic, or representational, image that bears some resemblance to its mythic subject; or an aniconic form that merely symbolizes the deity.

In a large number of celebrated shrines in India there are no beautiful statues of the gods and goddesses to be found, rather only aniconic blocks of stone or stumps of wood. This tradition of aniconic images derives from the rural folk religions of ancient India and bears witness to the great antiquity of the sanctity of certain places. The shrine in its initial phase may have been only a crude little hut covering a stone that both represented and contained some spirit of the natural world. As millennia passed and the small rural village slowly grew into a larger and larger town, both the myths concerning the stone and the shrine surrounding that stone were richly elaborated. It is therefore important when studying or visiting the monumental pilgrimage shrines of India to remember that many of them had their architectural genesis in the simple nature sanctuaries of the archaic rural folk.

The myths and legends of these sacred places have their roots in the ancient peoples' felt experience of the characteristics or qualities of the natural place. The various mythological personality characteristics of the deities in pilgrimage shrines may therefore be interpreted as metaphors for the way in which the spirit of the place has affected human beings. This spirit of place is not just a fanciful story, it is an actuality, an energy, a presence that touches human beings and affects them profoundly. Why are certain places said to be the dwelling place of a feminine deity and others the dwelling place of a masculine deity? Is it not perhaps because some ancient rural people, deeply in touch with the earth as a living entity, sensed either a feminine or masculine presence at a place and spoke about it in anthropomorphic terms? These terms were then given representational form by the artistic rendering of a statue or image.

Looking deeper into this matter, let us then ask why there are not simply male and female deities but, more precisely, why there are different kinds of male and female deities? Conventional explanations refer to such things as the fanciful human imagination, the rich and varied proto-religious inputs into formative Hinduism, and prehistoric deification of charismatic human figures into legendary archetypes. While all these things did occur, they are not the only explanations. The central premise of my theory is that the different personality characteristics of the deities derive from the various characteristics of the Earth spirit as it manifests at different geographical locations. To understand the quality, character or power of a specific place, we need only study the nature of the deity enshrined there. Encoded in the deity's mythological form is a clear message indicating how a particular sacred site may affect us.

banaras

Banaras is the most visited pilgrimage destination in all of India. One of the seven Holy Cities, one of the twelve Jyotir Linga sites and also a Shakti Pitha site, it is the most favored place for Hindus to die and be cremated. Myths and hymns speak of the waters of the Ganges River as the fluid medium of Shiva's divine essence and a bath in the river is believed to wash away all of one's sins. The particular river-side location of Banaras is considered especially potent because, in less than six miles (ten kilometers), the Ganges is met by two other rivers, the Asi and the Varana. Commenting of this specific location of Banaras along the river Ganges, the Hindu scripture Tristhalisetu explains that,

There whatever is sacrificed, chanted, given in charity, or suffered in penance, even in the smallest amount, yields endless fruit because of the power of that place. Whatever fruit is said to accrue from many thousands of lifetimes of asceticism, even more than that is obtainable from but three nights of fasting in this place.

Known in different eras as Avimukta, Varanasi and Kashi, meaning "where the supreme light shines", this great north Indian center of Shiva worship has had more than 3000 years of continuous habitation. Few standing buildings are older than the 16th century, however, as Muslim armies raiding from the 11th century onward destroyed the ancient Hindu temples and erected mosques on their foundations. Qutbuddin Aibak's armies were said to have destroyed more than a thousand temples in 1194, and Shah Jahan, the builder of the Taj Mahal, had seventy-six temples demolished. The city's primary Shiva shrine, the Jyotir Linga Visvanatha or 'Golden Temple', was rebuilt in 1776 across the road from its original location (now occupied by the Jnana Vapi mosque). Adjacent to this mosque is the Jnana Vapi well, the ritual center and axis mundi of Banaras. The Jnana Vapi, or Well of Wisdom, is said to have been dug by Shiva himself, and its waters carry the liquid form of Jhana, the light of wisdom. The imposing Alamgir mosque stands on the site of another of Kashi's most ancient and sacred shrines, the temple of Bindu Madhava.

In Hindu Kashi, it is said there are thirty-three hundred million shrines and a half a million images of the deities. Since a pilgrim would need all the years of his or her life to visit each of these shrines, it is considered wise to come to the holy city and never again leave. While this enormous number of shrines is perhaps a trifle exaggerated, Kashi does indeed have many hundreds of beautiful temples. Some of these temples are named after the great tirthas, or pilgrimage centers, in other parts of India - Rameshvaram, Dwarka, Puri, and Kanchipuram, for example - and it is said that merely by visiting Kashi one automatically gains the benefit of visiting all other sacred places. Most pilgrims make only short visits of days or weeks to Kashi, while others come to spend their remaining years in the holy city. Those who come to live in Kashi with the intention of dying there are called jivan muktas meaning those who 'are liberated while still alive'.

Kashi is also traditionally called Mahashamshana, 'the great cremation ground'. Hindus believe that cremation at the holy city insures moksha, or 'final liberation of the soul from the endless cycle of birth, death, and rebirth'. Because of this belief, dying persons and dead bodies from far-off places are brought to Kashi for cremation at the Manikarnika and other cremation sites (five principal and eighty-eight minor cremation/bathing sites lie along the Ganges). In her book, Banaras: City of Light, Diana Eck writes:

"Death in Kashi is not a feared death, for here the ordinary God of Death, frightful Yama, has no jurisdiction. Death in Kashi is death known and faced, transformed and transcended."

Encircling the holy city at a radius of five miles is the sacre d path known as the Panchakroshi Parikrama. Pilgrims take five days to circumambulate Kashi on this fifty-mile path, visiting 108 shrines along the way. If one is unable to walk the entire path a visit to the Panchakroshi Temple will suffice. By walking round the sanctuary of this shrine, with its 108 wall reliefs of the temples along the sacred way, the pilgrim makes a symbolic journey around the sacred city. Another important Banaras pilgrimage route is the Nagara Pradakshina, which takes two days to complete and has seventy-two shrines.

Today, a crowded, bustling, noisy, dirty city, Banaras was in antiquity an area of gently rolling hills, lush forests, and natural springs bordered by the magical waters of the river Ganges. A favored hermitage site for many of India's most venerated sages - Guatama Buddha and Mahavira, Kabir and Tulsi Das, Shankaracharaya, Ramanuja and Patanjali all meditated here - Banaras has been and continues to be one of the most visited holy places on the planet. First-time visitors to Banaras may find themselves initially overwhelmed by sensory stimulation, yet just beneath the surface is a presence of peacefulness and spiritual wisdom.

Readers interested in studying Banaras in greater detail are encouraged to consult the writings of Diana Eck, Roger Housden, Savitri Kumar, and Rana Singh listed in the India bibliography.

kumbh mela

Sacred site festivals in India, called melas, are a vital part of the pilgrimage tradition of Hinduism. Celebrating a mythological event in the life of a deity or an auspicious astrological period, the melas attract enormous numbers of pilgrims from all over the country. The greatest of these, the Kumbha Mela, is a riverside festival held four times every twelve years, rotating between Allahabad at the confluence of the Ganges, Yamuna and Saraswati rivers; Nasik on the Godavari River; Ujjain on the Sipra River; and Hardwar on the Ganges River. Bathing in these rivers during the Kumbha Mela is considered an endeavor of great merit, cleansing both body and spirit. The Allahabad and Hardwar festivals are routinely attended by five million or more pilgrims (13 million visited Allahabad in 1977, 18 million in 1989, and nearly 24 million in 2001) thus the Kumbha Mela is the largest religious gathering in the world. It also one of the oldest.

Two traditions are in circulation regarding the origin and timing of the festival: one that stems from ancient texts known as the Puranas, and the other that connects it with astrological considerations. According to the Puranic epic, the gods and demons had churned the milky ocean at the beginning of time in order to gather various divine treasures including a jar containing amrita, the nectar of immortality. As the jar emerged from the ocean the gods and demons began a terrific battle for its possession. For twelve days and twelve nights (equivalent to twelve human years) the gods and demons fought in the sky for the possession of the potion of immortality. During the battle, which according to some legends the gods won by trickery, four drops of the precious potion fell to earth. These places became the sites of the four Kumbha Mela festivals. The astrological tradition (ascribed to a lost Puranic text and not traceable in existing editions) seems to derive from a very ancient festival called the Kumbha Parva, which occurred at Hardwar every twelfth year when Jupiter was in Aquarius and the sun entered Aries. At some later time the term 'Kumbha' was prefixed to the melas held at Nasik, Ujjain and Prayaga (the earlier name of Allahabad), and these four sites became identified with the four mythical locations of the immortality potion. In theory the Kumbha Mela festivals are supposed to occur every three years, rotating between the four cities. In practice the four-city cycle may actually take eleven or thirteen years and this because of the difficulties and controversies in calculating the astrological conjunctions. Furthermore, the interval between the Kumbha Mela at Nasik and that at Ujjain is not of three years; they are celebrated the same year or only a year apart. This deviation in practice is intriguing and can not be fully explained by either astrological or mythological means. The following chart gives the astrological periods of the four melas, and the years of their most recent and future occurrences:

Hardwar.....when Jupiter is in Aquarius and the Sun is in Aries during the Hindu month of Caitra (March-April); 1986, 1998, 2010, 2021.

Allahabad.....when Jupiter is in Aries or Taurus and the Sun and Moon are in Capricorn during the Hindu month of Magha (January-February); 1989, 2001, 2012, 2024.

Nasik.....when Jupiter and the Sun are in Leo in the Hindu month of Bhadrapada (August-September); 1980, 1992, 2003, 2015.

Ujjain.....when Jupiter is in Leo and the Sun is in Aries, or when Jupiter, the Sun, and the Moon are in Libra during the Hindu month of Vaisakha (April-May); 1980, 1992, 2004, 2016.

The antiquity of the Kumbha Mela is shrouded in mystery. The Encyclopedia Britannica states that the Chinese Buddhist pilgrim, Hsuan Tsang, made a visit to an Allahabad festival in the 7th century AD while in the company of the King

Harsavardhana. Tradition associates the 9th century philosopher Sankaracharaya with the organization of the Kumbha Mela at Prayaga (Allahabad). Sankaracharaya had established four monasteries in the north, south, east and west of India, and had called upon yogis, sadhus and sages to meet at these sites for an exchange of philosophical views. These sites in the four cardinal directions were separated by great distances, however, and therefore the more centrally located site of Prayaga became the meeting place of choice. Indologists speculate that during the 9th to 12th centuries other monks and religious reformers perpetuated this periodic assemblage of sadhus and householders at sacred places on the banks of holy rivers, in order to create an environment of mutual understanding amongst different religious sects. Additionally, the festival gave householders the opportunity to benefit from their association with the normally reclusive sages and forest yogis. What was originally a regional festival at Prayaga thus became the preeminent pan-Indian pilgrimage site.

While many millions of Indians, male and female, young and old, lay person and monk, visit the Allahabad Kumbha Mela, the festival is traditionally known as the mela of ascetics and sadhus. At the most auspicious hour on the most auspicious day of the month-long festival many thousands of naked holy men from various sects will immerse themselves in the river for a ceremonial bath. Following the bathing of the sadhus, millions of other people attempt to enter the river. For a devout Hindu, to bathe at the Kumbha Mela sites (especially Allahabad and Hardwar) at this auspicious time is considered an opportunity of immeasurable significance. This great religious fervor of so many people focused on so small an area of land and water has frequently resulted in hundreds of pilgrims being trampled to death as the masses surge towards the river banks. During the 1954 Kumbha at Allahabad over 500 pilgrims were killed. The Indian government has taken measures to address this problem yet little can be done when such great numbers of pilgrims are involved.

Furthermore, it is important to note that many Hindus consider the Kumbha Mela sites to be the most favored places at which to die, and ritual suicide, though discouraged by the government, is still practiced. Westerners are bewildered, even shocked, by this matter and frequently make judgments without understanding the mythological, religious and cultural reasons behind the behavior. While it is beyond the scope of this essay to discuss the subject in detail, it is interesting to focus attention upon the two origin myths of the Kumbha Mela festival. Four drops of a nectar or potion of immortality were supposed to have fallen to earth at these sites, and at particular astrological periods the four sites are believed to function as portals into immortality and everlasting union with god. How did such myths arise and what is the message encoded in them? Perhaps there is some energy, some mysterious spirit or power, manifest at these places and times that somehow assists human beings to more fully experience spiritual immortality and divinity. The fact that hundreds of millions of people (coming from the most ancient and sophisticated philosophical and metaphysical system on earth) have for thousands of years believed this to be true suggests that an awesome power is indeed present at the Kumbha Mela sites.

In the case of those who give up their bodies after purifying themselves at Prayaga by bathing at the confluence of these two rivers – Ganga and Yamuna – the two wives of the ocean, there is no bondage of another body in a future birth and this liberation is achieved even without philosophical knowledge.

-Raghuvamsa 13-58

Pushkar temple

The description of pilgrimage places in the Tirtha-Yatra section of India's great epic, the Mahabharata, suggests a grand tour of the entire country. The pilgrimage begins in Pushkar, sacred to the god Brahma, and continues in a rambling clockwise direction throughout the subcontinent, ending in Prayaga (modern day Allahabad). As indicated by Pushkar's position as the starting point of the grand pilgrimage, the worship of Brahma was considered highly important at the end of the 1st millennium BC.

The common assumption of there being only one temple to Brahma is untrue. There are at least four major temples of the god still in use today. These are at Pushkar in Ajmer, Rajasthan; Dudhai in the state of Madhya Pradesh; Khed

Brahma in Kerala; and Kodakkal in the Malabar region of Kerala-Karnataka. Other deities have long eclipsed the cult of Brahma, and this waning of importance may be attributed to the fact that the function of Brahma - creating the world - has been completed, while Vishnu (the preserver) and Shiva (the destroyer) still have relevance to the continuing order of the universe.

Mythological literature describes Brahma as having sprung from the lotus originating in the navel of Vishnu. Brahma then becomes the source of all creation, the seed from which issues all space, time and causation. His consort Saraswati was manifested out of him and from their union were born all the creatures of the world. He is the inventor of theatrical art, and music and dance were revealed by him. He is sometimes depicted with four heads representing the four Vedas and the four Yugas (great epochs of time), and other times as Visvakarma, the divine architect of the universe. Saraswati is the wife of Brahma. Literally her name means 'the flowing one'. In the Rig Veda she represents a river deity and is connected with fertility and purification. She is considered the personification of all knowledge - arts, sciences, crafts and skills. She is the goddess of the creative impulse, the source of music, beauty and eloquence. Artists, writers and other individuals involved in creative endeavors have for millennia come on pilgrimage to Pushkar to request the inspiration of Brahma and Saraswati. According to the theory that shrine myths are often metaphorical expressions of the specific power of a pilgrimage place, the lake, hill and area of Pushkar have a spirit or presence that awakens and stimulates the human capacity of creativity.

There are five principal temples in Pushkar, all of relatively recent construction since the earlier buildings were destroyed by the Mugal emperor Aurangzeb in the late 17th century. Numerous bathing areas, known as ghats, surround the lake and pilgrims immerse themselves in the holy waters for a cleansing of both body and soul. During most of the year Pushkar is a small, quiet town. Each November, however, more than 200,000 people arrive, along with 50,000 cattle, for several days of pilgrimage, horse dealing, camel racing and colorful festivities.g waters, and others because of the association or habitation of saintly people.

Thiruvanamalai

In India there are three major categories of pilgrimage temples dedicated to the god Shiva: Jyotir Lingams; Svayambhu Lingams, and Bhuta Lingams. Located in five south Indian temples, the Bhuta Lingams are said to be places where Shiva manifested himself as the natural elements. The temples and their respective elements are Chidambaram: ether, Sri Kalahasti: wind, Tiruvanaikka/Jambunath: water, Kanchipuram: earth, and Tiruvanamalai: fire. Chidambaram is also associated with the heart, Tiruvanaikka with the stomach, and Tiruvanamalai with the chest.

An interesting legend, told in the excellent book Pilgrimage in the Hindu Tradition by Alan Morinis, tells how the sacred hill of Arunachala came to be associated with the fire Lingam of Shiva. Mourning the loss of his wife Sati, Shiva was wandering nude in the forests of Daruvana and was seen by the wives of certain sages. The women were aroused at the sight and desired to unite with him. The jealous sages cursed the god's linga (phallus) to fall off. As it touched the earth it grew to immense size like a great shining column. The gods Brahma and Vishnu saw it when its top had reached upwards beyond the clouds and its lower end was buried deep in the earth. They decided to investigate. Taking the form of a boar Vishnu dived into the depths of the primeval ocean to reach the base of the column, and Brahma taking the form of a swan flew up to its top. When they returned Vishnu honestly confessed that he could not find the foundations, while Brahma boasted that he had reached the summit. At this moment Shiva appeared, denounced Brahma as a liar, praised Vishnu for his honesty, and declared that the column could not be measured because it was his Linga. At the request of Vishnu, Shiva left part of his Linga in its 'tejas', or fire form, as the Arunachala hill.

The Arunachaleswar Shiva temple in Tiruvanamalai (Tiruvanamalai is the Tamil word for the Sanskrit Arunachala), situated at the foot of the Arunachala hill, is one of the largest (25 acres) and oldest temples in all of south India. The era of its founding is unknown; the complex grew over several millenia and the large towers, called gopurams, were erected between the 10th and 16th centuries. The tallest gopuram is over 60 meters tall and has 13 stories. The central temple enshrines images of Shiva as Lord Annamalai and his consort as

Unnamalai. Every year during the Hindu month of Kartikai (November-December), the great Deepam festival is held to celebrate Shiva's manifestation as the light of Arunachala. For ten days the whole city of Tiruvanamalai is alive with celebration, processions, dancing and singing. On the final day of the festival, the eve of the full moon, a huge beacon fire is lighted atop the hill in commemoration of the fire left by Shiva. Many thousands of pilgrims flock to this exciting festival from all over southern India. Arunachala hill is considered a miraculous healing place, especially for ailments of the lungs and barrenness in women. The hill of Arunachala is also a symbol of spiritual knowledge and several great sages ha

ve lived here, including Arunagirinathar, the author of the Tiruppugal, and Sri Ramana Maharshi (1879-1950).

Temples of Rameshvaram and Badrinath

The great Shiva temple of Rameshvaram, India

As discussed in the section, Introduction to the Pilgrimage Places of India, there are several ways in which pilgrimage sites are categorized in Hinduism. One of these concerns the four Dhamas, or the 'abodes' of the gods at the four directional compass points of India. While no specific legend explains the grouping of these four sites together, they were each highly regarded by the time of the Mahabharata (500 BC), they came to be listed together by the time of the early Puranas (4th century AD), and were given further emphasis in the 9th century when the great sage and scholar Sri Adi Sankara established monastic centers at them. The four Dhamas are: in the East, the Krishna temple of Jagannath in Puri, Orissa; in the North, the Vishnu temple in Badrinath, Uttar Pradesh; in the South, the Shiva temple of Rameshvaram in Tamil Nadu; in the West, the Krishna temple of Dwarka in Gujarat.

The temple at Rameshvaram, besides being considered a Dhama, is also one of the twelve sacred Jyotir Linga sites. These sites, located throughout the subcontinent of India, are where the god Shiva is said to have manifested as a towering column of fire. Among India's most ancient temples sites, they enshrine small pillars of stone, called lingas, which are worshipped as containing the creative power of Shiva. Unlike the other eleven Jyotir Linga sites, Rameshvaram has two sacred Lingas instead of just one. A legend from one of India's great epics, the Ramayana, explains this unique condition. A demon named Ravana had stolen Sita, the wife of Lord Rama. Following a terrific battle on the island of Lanka (modern day Ceylon or Sri Lanka) in which Rama killed the demon Ravana, Sita and Rama returned to India. At the site where they landed, Rama decided to install a Shiva Lingam to absolve him of the sin of destroying Ravana who, besides being a demon, was also a member of the Brahmin caste. Lord Rama sent his devotee, the monkey deity Hanuman, to Mt. Kailash to get a lingam from the god Shiva. Hanuman's journey took longer than expected, however, and as the auspicious time of worship neared, Sita quickly fashioned a lingam out of sand. When Hanuman finally arrived with a stone lingam from Kailash he was disappointed to find another lingam already installed. To please Hanuman, Rama installed the stone lingam beside the sand one and ordered that all worship should henceforth be given first to the Visvalingam brought by Hanuman, and only then to the Ramalinga made by Sita.

The enormous temple of the two Shiva Lingams lies near the seashore at the tip of India. Besides the 100-foot tall gopuram towers shown in the photograph, the temple is renowned for its magnificent corridors with massive stone pillars. Decorating the sides of the gopuram towers and throughout the interior of the temple are thousands of exquisite sculptures depicting mythic events from the Ramayana. There are also twenty-two sacred bathing pools within the temple complex. Fully clothed pilgrims immerse themselves in each of these pools - known for their miraculous healing cures - before praying at the two Shiva Lingams. Perhaps the finest example of Dravidian architecture in south India, the present temple dates from the 12th century and is the composite work of several different kings. More than ten thousand pilgrims pass through the temple each day, making Rameshvaram one of the most visited and vital sacred sites in all of Asia.

Town and temple complex of Badrinath

The holy Dhama temple of Badrinath, far north from Rameshvaram's seaside location, is in the state of Uttar Pradesh, in the Uttarkhand region of the Himalaya mountains. Perched above the Alaknanda River, a headstream of the Ganges, the temple's elevation is 10,248 feet (3050meters). Because of the extreme cold of the high mountain winter the shrine is only open in the summer months. When the first snows fall the sacred statue of Vishnu (seated in the Yogic padmasana pose) is clothed in a thick woolen blanket, the temple is closed and locked, and the priests move down the mountain to the town of Joshimath for the winter. Badrinath has been a well known pilgrimage site for over 2000 years and the Buddhist architectural influence in the shrine shows that Badrinath has also been venerated by Buddhists since very early times. Immediately adjacent to the shrine is the hot spring pool of Taptakund in which pilgrims take a dip before worshipping Sri Badrinatha.

...Mercury

Tiruchendur........Jupiter

Srirangam...........Venus

Tirunallaru..........Saturn

Dwarka

Jagatmandir temple, Dwarka, India

Among India's many different pilgrimage sites, particular ones are traditionally viewed as being especially holy for a variety of different mythological reasons. Preeminent among this listing are the Sapta Puri or Seven Sacred Cities and the four Dhamas or "Divine Abodes" (for more information on the Dhamas, see the photos and text for Rameshvaram, on this web site). The Seven Sacred Cities of Ayodhya, Mathura, Haridwar, Banaras, Kanchi, Ujjain and Dwarka are known as Mokshada, meaning 'Bestower of Liberation', and these sites are believed to confer liberation upon all persons who die within their boundaries. Dwarka, one of these seven sacred cities, is also listed among the Four Divine Abodes.

Seldom visited by westerners because of its remote location in the western state of Gujarat, the fascinating and extremely beautiful Jagatmandir temple is bordered on one side by the ocean coast and on the other side by the town of Dwarka. One of India's oldest and most venerated pilgrimage sites, Dwarka's archaeological and historical background is shrouded in mystery. Mythologically, Dwarka - or Dvaravati as it is known in Sanskrit - was the site chosen by Garuda, the Divine Eagle, who brought Krishna here when he departed Mathura. Krishna founded the beautiful city and lived there the remaining years of his life until he died (according to legend) in 3102 BC. Scholars confer that the oldest parts of the Jagatmandir temple may only date to the reconstructions of the Gupta period in 413 AD.

In the 7th century the sage Shankaracharya established four great monasteries in the cardinal directions of the country (Sringeri in the south, Puri in the east, Joshimath in the north, and Dwarka in the west). This emphasis on Dwarka further increased its importance as a pilgrimage destination. The original temples were destroyed during the 11th century by Muslim armies; frequently rebuilt, they continued to be attacked by the Muslims through the 15th century. The existing temple of Jagatmandir, also known as Sri Dwarkadish, dates from a 1730 rebuilding. It is 52 meters tall, and enshrines an idol called Sri Ranchhodrayji. The temple stands five storeys tall and is built on 72 pillars.

Students of the science of archaeoastronomy will recognize significance in this number 72, one of the most important numbers in the so-called 'precessional code' (re)discovered by the scholars Santillana and von Dechend. The astronomical phenomenon of precession concerns the very slow wobble of the axis of the earth and its effect for earth-bound observers of a gradual and cyclical slippage of the belt of the zodiac against the rising point of the sun. This precessional slippage operates at the rate of one degree every 72 years and means that each constellation houses the sun for an average of 2160 years. All twelve constellations take 25,920 years to pass completely through the cycle. These numbers of 72, 2160, 25,920 and various permutations of them have been shown by Santillana and von Dechend, in their book Hamlet's Mill, to be mysteriously present in ancient myths and sacred architecture all around the world. While little archaeoastronomical study of Jagatmandir temple has so far been conducted, the presence of the number 72 in so important a part of the temple's architecture suggests that future studies will result in many fascinating revelations.

Besides being a Sapta Puri, a Dhama, and a Shankaracharya Mutt, Dwarka is also visited by large numbers of pilgrims because of its association with the great bhakti saint Mira Bai. One of India's most popular saints, Mira Bai renounced her splendid life as the wife of a powerful 16th century king to dedicate her days to the worship of Lord Krishna. Mira Bai followed the spiritual path known as Bhakti Yoga, which is characterized by a devotional love of god. Much easier to practice (and perhaps more efficient at producing spiritual enlightenment) than other yogic methods which require textual study and great discipline, Bhakti Yoga is the primary religious method of India's teeming masses. The path of the Bhakti yogi is essentially the practice of invoking the presence of the divine through adoration of a statue, icon or painting of a deity. In Mira Bai's case, as with many other saints in India's long history, this invocation called forth not only the felt presence of the deity but actually a living, moving form of Krishna. Similar to the physical apparitions of Mary and Christ to devoted Christians, Krishna visited Mira Bai to eat, sing, dance and play with her. Mira Bai lived the final years of her life in Dwarka and there wrote to Krishna her immortal poems of love. Krishna, the preeminent devotional deity in Hinduism is venerated here and legions of bhakti yogis such as Mira Bai have infused the temple with a power of love. The pilgrimage shrine of Jagatmandir in Dwarka is thus highly charged with the quality or energy of devotion and will awaken and amplify that quality in visiting pilgrims.

Ancient legends of Dwarka tell that the holy city was long ago entirely swept away by a great wave of water. This legend, disregarded by contemporary historians and archaeologists, has recently been given credence by findings of the new science of inundation mapping, which produces accurate models of ancient shorelines at specific dates. The legend has been given further support by oceanographic studies which have pr

oven the existence of submerged temple structures off the coast of Dwarka.

Other sacred sites associated with Krishna are Mathura, Vrindivana, Gokula, Barsana, Govardhana and Kuruksetra.

Vrindavan

Painting of Krishna and Radha on temple wall, Vrindavan

Painting of Krishna and Radha on temple wall, Vrindavan

Located on the banks of the Yamuna River in the state of Uttar Pradesh, the town of Vrindavan is the site of an ancient forest where the Hindu deity Krishna spent his childhood days. Approximately 15 kilometers from Mathura, the city of Krishna's birthplace, the town has hundreds of temples dedicated to the worship of Krishna and his consort Radha.

Krishna, an incarnation of Lord Vishnu, was born in the long ago era of the Dwapara Yuga as the eighth son of the Yadava prince Vasudev and his wife

Devaki. To save him from the murderous intentions of his maternal uncle Kansa, Krishna was taken soon after birth to Gokul, the village of cowherds in Vrindavan. There he was raised in the care of his foster parents Nanda Maharaj and Yasoda.

Krishna, Radha and a dancing Gopi, Vrindavan

Krishna, Radha and a dancing Gopi, Vrindavan

A Hindu scripture, the Bhagavata Purana, describes Krishna's childhood pastimes in the Vrindavan forest where he, his brother Balarama and his cowherd friends engaged in youthful pranks. Krishna danced with the local girls known as gopis, hid their clothes while they bathed, spread the message of divine love with his lover Radha, and subdued various demons. These pastimes were the source of inspiration for the famous 13th century poem, Gita Govinda, by the Sanskrit poet, Jayadeva.

It is believed that the spiritual essence of Vrindavan was lost over time until the great saint Chaitanya Mahaprabhu rediscovered it. In the year 1515, Chaitanya visited Vrindavana, and wandering through the sacred forests located the holy places associated with Krishna's divine actions.

Hindu priest with statues of Krishna and Gopis, Vrindavan

Hindu priest with statues of Krishna and Gopis, Vrindavan

Vrindavan is an important Hindu pilgrimage site, especially for the followers of the Vaishnava tradition, which maintains numerous temples and monastic dwellings known as ashrams. Many millions of devotees of Krishna and Radha visit these places of pilgrimage every year and participate in colorful festivals that relate to the scenes from Krishna's life.

One of the most important temples is the Govinda Deo, built in 1590. Other popular temples include: Madan Mohan, Banke Bihari, Radha Vallabh, Jaipur, Jaigurudeo, Sri Radha Raman, Shahji, Rangaji, Govinda Deo, Sri Krishna-

Balarama, Radha Damodar, Shri Maa Katyayni, Chintaharan Hanuman, Shree Radha Ras Bihari Ashta Sakhi, Kesi Ghat and Seva Kunj.

Vrindavan is also known as the City for Widows because of the thousands of widows who seek refuge there. By Hindu tradition, widows may not remarry but should devote their remaining years to spiritual liberation. Some widows leave their families after the death of their husbands (or their families leave them) and make their way to the holy city of Vrindavan. In exchange for singing sacred hymns known as bhajans in the temples these women are given meals and a little money.

Tirumala

Venkateshwara Temple, Tirumala

Venkateshwara Temple, Tirumala

Tirumala, a hill town located in the state of Andhra Pradesh, 573 kilometers (356 miles) southeast of the capital Hyderabad, is the most visited Hindu pilgrimage sites in all of India. Its nationwide fame is due to the magnificent temple of Sri Venkateswara, a deity also known as Shrimann Narayana, Maha Vishnu, Srinivasa and Balaji.

Tirumala is a combination of two words: Tiru means 'holy' or 'sacred' and Mala means 'hills' or 'mountain' in the Tamil language, therefore Tirumala translates as Holy Mountains. There are in fact seven peaks and the temple of Venkateswara is situated on the seventh peak called Venkatadri. Venkateswara means Lord of the Venkata Hill and he is also called the Lord of the Seven Hills. In Sanskrit the name Venkateswara can be split into three parts: Vem (Destroy), Kata (Sin), and Ishwara (Supreme Lord). Using this etymology, Venkateswara refers to the Supreme Lord who destroys sins.

According to the Hindu scriptures, Vishnu, out of love towards his devotees, incarnated as Venkateswara and appeared for the salvation and upliftment of humanity. He is considered the Supreme form of Vishnu in this age. It is said that Kubera, the Lord of Wealth, lent money to Venkateswara for his marriage with the goddess Padmavati (an incarnation of Lakshmi, the goddess of wealth and good fortune). In remembrance of this, the devotees donate money and gold to Venkateswara so that he can repay Lord Kubera.

The center of the temple complex is a monumental tower with a golden roof. Its inner temple houses the main deity, Lord Sri Venkateswara. The deity stands directly beneath a golden dome and is believed to be self-manifested because no human being is known to have installed it in the shrine. The statue wears a golden crown, which is embedded with a large emerald (supposedly the largest in the world) as well as many diamonds and other jewels. On special occasions, it is replaced with a diamond crown. Venkateswara has a dark complexion and four hands. In his two upper hands he holds a discus (a symbol of power) and a conch shell (a symbol of existence). With his lower hands extended downward he asks devotees to have faith and surrender to him for protection. Venkateswara's eyes are covered because it is said that his gaze is so intense it would scorch the universe.

The temple of Sri Venkateswara has acquired unique sanctity in Indian religious lore. The Sastras, Puranas and numerous other scriptures declare that one can attain enlightenment only by worshipping Venkateswara. All the great dynasties of rulers of the southern peninsula have paid homage to Venkateswara, including the Pallavas of Kanchipuram (9th century AD), the Cholas of Thanjavur (a century later), the Pandyas of Madurai, and the kings and chieftains of Vijayanagar (14th - 15th century AD). After the decline of the Vijayanagar dynasty, nobles and chieftains from all parts of the country continued to pay their homage and offer gifts to the temple.

The temple attracts approximately 80,000 to 100,000 pilgrims every day – forty million a year - and devotees will wait in long lines for ten or more hours in order to view the statue for less than two seconds. Devotees donate money to

Venkateswara and the amounts received average $400,000 per day. Many devotees offer gold as a token of their love and these gold offering average 3000 kilograms (6500 pounds) per year. The annual income, estimated at 185 million dollars in 2008, runs charitable trusts, schools, hospitals and the feeding of the many millions of pilgrims visiting the shrine The Tirumala temple is believed to be the richest of all the temples in the world and the jewel studded statue to be the single most valuable object on the planet.

Many devotees have their heads shaved as an offering to Venkateswara. The amount of hair collected each day is over one ton. The hair is sold by the temple organization to international buyers for use as hair extensions and in cosmetics, bringing over $6 million to the temple's treasury each year.

The town celebrates most Vaishnava (Vishnu) festivals with great splendor, while the Brahmotsavam celebrated every year during September is the most important festival and receives millions of devotees over the short span of a week. Other major festivals include Vasanthotsavam (spring festival), conducted in March–April, and Rathasapthami (Magha Shuddha Saptami), celebrated in February, when Lord Venkateswara's deity is taken on procession around the temple chariots.

The Venkateswara temple is one of the three Archavathara Vishnu temples, the others being at Srirangam and Badrinath, and also one of the 108 Divya Desam Vishnu temples. Other important temples in the Tirumala region include Srikalahasti, Srinivasa Mangapuram, Sri Padmavati Devi Alayam, Govinda Raja Swami, Kodanda Rama Swami, Kapileswara Swami and Kalyana Venkateswara.

Jyotir Linga Shiva Temples

Shiva Linga and painting of Shiva, Tanjore temple

Tamil Nadu, India

Of the three gods of the Hindu trinity, Shiva is the most commonly worshipped in India today, Vishnu being the second, and Brahma the third. The origins of Shiva are found in a pre-Aryan fertility god and also in a fierce deity of the Vedas called Rudra. Shiva is a god of many and often contrasting characteristics. He is associated with the creative energy of the universe, and at the same time with its destruction. Literally his name means 'One in whom the universe sleeps after destruction and before the next cycle of creation'. It is said that all that is created must one day disintegrate; this disintegration is a return to the formless void from which creation may once again spring forth. Shiva is the dynamic power behind this endless cycle of birth, death, and rebirth.

He is the master of Tantric yoga, an esoteric science of sexuality, and also the Lord of ascetics, renunciates and yogis. He is the god of the battlefield, the cremation grounds, and inauspicious crossroads. Demons, ghosts, and evil spirits are believed to sometimes accompany him. Frequently a frightening deity, Shiva is also the exponent of the arts and the creator of dance.

Shiva may be worshipped in both his anthropomorphic form, as a statue of a man, or more commonly in his aniconic form, the linga. The word linga means sign or mark and it is understood to be the symbolic representation of the creative and destructive energies of Shiva. In some temples the Linga is simply an un-sculpted outcropping of stone two to three feet tall; in others a similarly sized round pillar has been made and installed. These pillars will usually have two defined parts: a circular horizontal base called a yoni or a pitha, which is the female component, and the vertical stone shaft signifying the Shiva component (there may also be a square base signifying Brahma and an octagonal one signifying Vishnu). Sometimes the face of Shiva may be carved or painted upon the linga, or there may be a serpent, a common symbol of Shiva.

Contrary to the common, though inaccurate, notion held in the West, Hindus do not worship the Shiva Lingam as a phallic image. Prudish Christian missionaries made this mistaken claim in the 18th century. The real explanation for linga worship is the same as for similar types of standing stones and sacred mountains throughout the world. These objects are understood to be the sources or dwelling places of the spirits of the earth.

Shiva temples are abundant throughout India's many thousands of cities and villages, yet only a small number of these temples are places of pilgrimage. This distinction arises from the fact that, while any structure may house an idol of Shiva, and thereby be used in the worship of the deity, true pilgrimage shrines are those places where Shiva has actually manifested some aspect of his divine nature. Hindu texts delineate three distinct categories of Shiva shrines: the Jyotir Lingas, the Bhuta Lingas, and the Swayambhu Lingas. The Jyotir Lingas, twelve in number and located throughout the country, are considered the most important. They are:

Grineshwar in Visalakam, near the Ellora caves, Maharashtra

Somnath in Saurashtra, Gujarat

Mahakalaswar at Ujjain, Madhya Pradesh

Amareswara at Omkareshwar on the river Narmada, Madhya Pradesh

Tryambakesvara near Nasik on the river Godvari, Maharashtra

Naganath, in Daruka Vanam, Maharashtra

Vaidyanath at Deogarh, Bihar

Bhimasankar northwest of Poona, in Dhakini, Maharashtra, (sometimes alternately listed as a shrine near Gauhati, Assam)

Kedarnath in the Utterkhand Himalaya, Uttar Pradesh

Viswanath at Banaras/Varanasi, Uttar Pradesh

Malikarjuna at Srisailam, Andhra Pradesh state, (also a Shakti Pitha site)

Rameshvaram, Tamil Nadu

The five Bhuta Lingas are places where Shiva is said to have manifested himself as a Linga of a natural element.

Chidambaram: Ether

Sri Kalahasti: Wind

Tiruvanaikka/Jambunath: Water

Kanchipuram: Earth

Tiruvanamalai: Fire

The Swayambhu Linga temples contain representations of Shiva that are believed to have risen up by themselves in the primordial past. In the commentary by Nigamajnanadeva on his Jirnoddharadasakam, sixty-eight Swayambhu Lingas are listed along with commentary. For further information and a listing of these sites, consult Gopinatha Rao in the bibliography.

Srisailam and Shakti Pitha shrines

Stone carving showing serpent form of Shiva and goddess Shakti at Srisailam temple,

Andhra Pradesh state, India

Located on the side of the ancient sacred hill of Srigiri, in the Nallamalai range of Andhra Pradesh, is the exotic temple of Srisailam. The temple complex, whose existing buildings date from the 2nd century AD, is one of the twelve Jyotir Linga Shiva shrines as well as one of the eighteen most sacred goddess shrines, or Shakti Pithas. This unique combination of major god and goddess shrines at the same site makes Srisailam one of India's most holy sites. Shiva is worshipped here in his form of Lord Mallikarjuna, and Shakti, his consort, as Sri Bharamaramba Devi. The images of these deities, both extremely old, are enshrined in the more recent temple built by the Vijayanager king Harihara Raya around 1404 AD. The temple, whose popular name is Sriparvata, is surrounded by a great fortress-like wall, which is 20 feet high, 6 feet wide and 2120 feet in circumference. Built in in 1520 AD, the wall has 3200 stones, each weighing over one ton, and is decorated with fine relief carvings depicting scenes from Hindu mythology.

Goddess worship occurred in India since deepest antiquity and clearly predates the Indus Valley Harappan civilization (3000 BC). Worship of the goddess in her many forms occurs all over the sub-continent and in many places she is more popular than the gods Shiva or Vishnu. All the goddesses of Hinduism are considered to be manifestations of the multi-faceted personality of the one great Mother Goddess of creation. According to certain Hindu myths, the goddess is the combined energy of all the gods, who created and then equipped her with weapons so that she might destroy a demon whose power was greater than theirs. Different temples will enshrine different images of the goddess, from her peaceful aspects of Parvati, Lakshmi, and Saraswati, to her fearful aspects of Durga, Chamunda and Kali; she is both the gentle giver of life and the terrible mistress of death. Worshipped by particular sects of Hinduism known as Tantric, the goddess encourages meditation on yantras (visual mantras considered to be magic diagrams), erotic sexual practices, and the ritual slaughter of animals. Before her shrines at many Shakti Pitha sites are large, two-pronged forks for securing the heads of animals being sacrificed. In the active Shakti Pitha shrines at least one goat will be sacrificed daily and on major festival days several hundred goats and many buffaloes will be slaughtered. Pilgrims passing the place of sacrifice will dip a finger in the blood and touch it to their lips and foreheads. The background idea here is not that the goddess is cruel, but that she is looked upon as the protectress from all evil, ailment, danger and death. She should frighten away the demons and sorcerers of misfortune. In her terrible aspects she also confronts pilgrims with the transience of life and death, thereby encouraging them to seek eternal wisdom and enlightenment.

The primary sacred places of the goddess are the Shakti Pithas and they are variously described in different texts as being 18, 51, 52 or 108 in number, each of these sites being associated with a particular part of Shakti's body. A fascinating legend (recounted from Pilgrimage in the Hindu Tradition, by Alan Morinis) gives insight into the miraculous healing powers of the Shakti Pithas. Shakti is the daughter of Daksa and Prasuti, and the wife of Shiva. Daksa once decided to hold a great sacrifice to which he invited neither his daughter nor son-in-law. Shakti was offended by this slight and attended the sacrifice uninvited. There she was insulted by Daksa and, thus humiliated, she took her life. On hearing this news, her husband Shiva hastened to the house of Daksa, disrupted the sacrifice, killed Daksa, and claimed the body of his wife. Inconsolable at his loss, he placed Shakti's body on his shoulder and began a mad dance through the three universes. His dance threatened to destroy all creation and the gods became distraught at this prospect. One version of the story has it that the gods approached Vishnu to restrain Shiva. Vishnu sent arrows or his discus to dismember the body of Shakti limb by limb. An alternative version states that Brahma, Vishnu and Sani entered Shakti's body and caused it to disintegrate. When Shiva was thereby deprived of the body, he ceased his mad dance. The parts of Shakti's body fell from Shiva's shoulders to the earth, and the places where they landed became the sacred Shakti Pithas. For countless centuries these sites have been visited by women having ailments in certain parts of their bodies - the temple enshrining a particular part of Shakti's body is believed to have the miraculous capacity to heal that same part of a woman's body. Some of the Shakti Pithas are also called Siddha-Pithas because they are considered highly effective for the acquisition of spiritual powers; at these sites, Srisailam being one of them, the goddess is known to confer wisdom, bliss and enlightenment.

The names and locations of the Shakti Pithas are too long to give here. Readers interested in learning more about these places can consult books by Bagchi, Housden, Morinis, Sastri, and Sircar listed in the bibliography. A good listing of the 51 Shakti Pithas is given in Travels through Sacred India by Roger Housden, and directions to these shrines may be found in the guidebook entitled India, by John Howley.

Muruga Shrines of South India

Muruga Swamimalai

Temple priest and statue of Muruga at Paramthirsolai Tamil Nadu, India

In the southern Indian state of Tamil Nadu, the 'Six Homes of Lord Muruga' are among the most colorful, exotic and vital pilgrimage sites in the world. Muruga, or Murukan, is the Tamil name for a god who is also known as Skanda, Subrahmanya, Kumara and Kartikeya; he is an amalgamation of two deities, deriving from ancient indigenous Tamil culture and external Vedic influences. In Epic times, myths of the Mahabharata and Ramayana describe Skanda as a celestial warrior-hero born of the seed of the god Rudra for the purpose of defeating troublesome demons known as Asuras. This Skanda of the Epics, when he is brought into Tamil Nadu, becomes linked with Murukan, a name originally given to a god of the Kurincis culture. The Kurincis, a folk people living in the forested hills, had a legendary love of dance, play and nature, and the name of their god Murukan means 'beautiful, fragrant, young and vibrant one'. References in Tamil poetry of the 1st and 2nd centuries AD describe Murukan as a lord of the hills and hunt, a controller of epidemics and malevolent forces, a deity who is fondly worshipped with the frenzied dance of beautifully adorned damsels. He is also a philosopher-teacher who is accepted as the inspiration and author of Tamil language and literature.

From a legendary time early in the 1st millenium BC, Murukan is already associated with six sacred hills, the myth of each site suggesting how he manifested himself there. Explanations for the number six are given by reference to the god's six qualities of felicity, fullness, immortal youth, limitless energy, protection from evil, and spiritual splendor. He is also associated with the six directions of east, west, north, south, up and down, as well the five primordial elements and the whole. An excellent and highly readable discussion of Muruga and his worship in Tamil Nadu is given in an article by Professor Fred Clothey in the Journal of the Academy of Religions (see bibliography); much of the following information on the six sites was taken from that article.

The Murukan devotees are unanimous in stating the existence of six sites yet only five of these sites are accepted as authentic without dispute. The first is Palani, some twenty miles from Dindigul Junction. At this place Muruga and his brother Ganesh were tested by their parents Shiva and Parvati. Whichever of the sons could most quickly travel around the cosmos would be given the gift of a rare fruit. Muruga, the younger and brasher, set off at a rapid pace to circle the world; Ganesh, the wiser, merely walked around his father Shiva. Returning from his arduous journey Muruga was humbled and, retreating to the the hill of Palani, he spent many years as an ascetic monk meditating and seeking wisdom. Palani is also associated with healing; this tradition being nurtured by local legends about bhogars or mystical alchemists who in a prehistoric era constructed the main icon of the Palani temple from a combination of nine different medicinal and immortalizing substances. Neither the age of this still existing icon is known nor the proportion of its ingrediants. Any substance that comes into contact with the icon is believed to acquire miraculous healing powers, and countless are the number of healings that have occurred within the temple.

The seaside shrine of Tiruchendur is the second major site. Its name means 'village of the sacred battle' and it is here where the young Muruga conquered the troublesome demon named Surapadman. When Muruga finally found the demon's dwelling place in a tree, he split the tree with his lance and the demon, rather than being killed, was turned into a radiantly lovely peacock that became the vehicle of Muruga. A fascinating festival celebrating Muruga's victory over the demonic forces is held at the Tiruchendur temple each October/November.

The third site is Tiruttani, some seventy-five miles northwest of Madras city. On this hill Muruga came for meditation and purification after his battle with the demons. It is where he ruled his domain from, where he conducted his courtship of a forest goddess, and where he taught as a philosopher. Tituttani, meaning 'blissful repose' is the scene of numerous bhajanais, or musical festivals, in which large numbers of pilgrims come to worship with devotional singing and dancing.

Tirupparankunram, a hill five miles southwest of Madurai, is the fourth pilgrimage site of Muruga. A cave temple dedicated to the element of earth and mentioned in various classical Tamil texts as the 'Southern Himalaya' where the gods assemble, Tirupparankunram is also mentioned in legend as 'the place where the sun and moon abide'. Muruga was married to Devasena upon the hill and for many centuries the Tamil people have considered it the most auspicious place for their own marriages, especially during the time of the Pankuni Uttiram, the festival of marriage held in late March. Besides the fantastic temple to Muruga on the hill, there is also a Muslim shrine dedicated to 'Sekunder', who is associated with Murukan by the Muslim pilgrims.

The fifth site, Swamimalai, meaning 'Mountain of the Lord' is near the city of Kunbakonam in Tanjavur district. It is here that the child Muruga taught his father Shiva the meaning of the sacred syllable 'OM'. The icon at Swamimalai depicts the boy Muruga perched on his father's shoulder whispering into his ear. The temple gopuram (great tower) is emblazoned with a neon 'OM'.

Regarding the identity of the sixth major site, there is no consensus among scholars and many local temples are ascribed the distinction. During the author's visit to the five shrines listed above, numerous temple priests were interviewed and asked for their opinion on the matter. The answer most often given was the shrine of Paramthirsolai, twelve miles east of Madurai (at the top of the hill of Alagar, above the Alagarcoil Vishnu temple). While this temple is not as large or bustling as the other five recognized shrines, it is just as incredible to visit, and for the author had the most mysterious atmosphere.

Sabarimala

Shayana Pradikshanam devotional practice of pilgrims at Sabarimala

In the Indian state of Kerala, only 10 degrees above the equator, is a land of steep mountains thickly covered with splendid tropical forests. The early people of this region, of a Dravidian ancestral stock, lived amongst the trackless valleys and roaring streams in small tribal groups. Farming little, they hunted in the teeming forests, and their primary deity, Ayappa, was a youthful forest god. Various legends explain the birth of Ayappa (also known as Dharmasasta). One begins with Shiva roaming the mountain kingdoms of the Himalayas. There he sees a lovely maiden and, overcome with desire, makes passionate love with her. But the maiden is married to another man, a tribal chieftain who vows revenge on the god. The tribal chieftain retires to an ice cave in the high mountains and practices austerities for a thousand years. Through these austerities he gains great psychic powers and finally goes forth to punish Shiva. From the heights of Mt. Kailash, Shiva sees the tribal chieftain approaching. The chieftain looks like a terrible demon and Shiva, overcome with fear, calls on the god Vishnu for assistance and protection. Vishnu manifests himself as a beautiful damsel, seduces the demon chieftain, and destroys him. But then Shiva, once again overcome with sexual desire, sees the radiant damsel (who is merely Vishnu in another form) and mates with her. Out of this union comes a baby boy named Ayappa. Embodying the qualities of both Vishnu and Shiva, Ayappa is an avatar (divinity in human form) born into the world to battle the demons of the hill tribes of Kerala. Shiva tells the magical child of his dharma-life (a life of service), and leaves him upon the bank of a mountain stream where he is discovered by a childless tribal king. Brought up by the king, Ayappa does many miracles, is a great healer and a defeater of demons. After fulfilling the purpose of his incarnation Ayappa entered the inner sanctum of the ancient temple upon sacred Mt. Sabari and disappeared. During his mythical life, Ayappa kept the company of tigers and leopards. Mystics living in the deep forests surrounding the Sabarimala Mountains have for a thousand years reported seeing Ayappa riding through the jungles upon a majestic tiger.

The shrine of Sabarimala is one of the most remote shrines in southern India yet it still draws three to four million pilgrims each year. Before beginning the multi-day walk through the mountain jungles to get to Sabarimala, the pilgrims prepare themselves with 41 days of rigorous fasting, celibacy, meditation and prayer. Finally arriving at the shrine, the pilgrims will wait in line for hours, even days, to have one or two seconds in front of the image of Ayappa. After seeing the deity, many pilgrims will complete a vow called Shayana Pradikshanam. In the Malayalam language of Kerala, Shayana means "body" and Pradakshinam means "revolution," so Shayana Pradakshinam means "revolution with the Body." This devotional practice is done not only in Sabarimala but also in other temples in Kerala.

The Sabarimala shrine is only open a few times each year: the Mandalam festival covering 41 days from November 15 to December 26; the Makaravilakku from January 1-14; on Vishu, the day of the vernal equinox in April; and during smaller festivals in May/June and August/September. The shrine, unlike many in southern India is open to persons of all religious callings, and there are no caste restrictions during the pilgrimage. However, women - unless they are younger than six or older than sixty - are not allowed to come to Sabarimala. This is explained by referring to the celibacy of Ayappa and the concern that he might be lured away from his shrine by a woman his age (if certain readers find this somewhat sexist, they are informed that there are particular goddess shrines in south India which men are forbidden to enter). It is said that during the pilgrimage periods no tigers are found along the forest trails leading to Sabarimala. This is explained as resulting from Ayappa's power over tigers. Other holy places associated with Ayappa are Kulattupuzha, Aryankavu, Accankovil, and Kantamala.

Additional notes on SABARIMALA and AYAPPA

The information given above was taken from different books on the Sabarimala shrine. After putting these writings on the web site, I received the following material from a reader of the web site, Geetha Krishnan. This new material, relating to the legend of Ayappa, is somewhat different than what I had written. This sort of difference in legend and myth is something quite common in the study of sacred places, and therefore I have included both versions of the Ayappa myth. Thank you to Geetha Krishnan for this alternative myth.

Shiva does not call upon Vishnu after mating with a tribal woman. The story goes that Shiva gives a boon to an asura (a demon) that allows him to merely touch a person on his head and he will fall dead. The asura then thanks him and wants to try out the boon on Lord Shiva himself. In fear, Shiva runs and calls upon Lord Vishnu for help. Lord Vishnu in the guise of the beautiful maiden Mohini, which literally means "enchantress" or "seductress", approaches the asura. She questions him about why he is chasing Shiva. The asura tells her how he has received this boon and wanted to test it on Shiva himself. Mohini tricks the foolish asura by telling him that the boon was really ineffective and Shiva did not want him to know that. If he wanted, he could test it on himself. The asura placed his hand on his own head, believing her, and he falls dead. Shiva is very grateful towards Vishnu but is enchanted by his female form. They have the child Ayappa to satisfy the demigods' plea to save them from the torments of the demon Mahishi. Ayappa is then raised by the King of Panthala, Rajashekharan, a truly royal king not a tribal king, who was childless. Right after adopting the child Ayappa, whom he called Mani Kanda, meaning 'one who wears a bell around his neck' (for the child was found wearing a small bell on a chain around his neck that attracted the king's attention who was out on a hunt with his men), the king has a child of his own. When Ayappa was about to reach age, the queen feared that her own child would lose his right to the throne, so with the minister of the court, she schemed to murder Ayappa. She faked being ill saying that her stomach was in unbearable pain. The minister bribed the court physician to say that the only remedy would be a female tiger's milk. Ayappa, willing to do anything for his mother, goes on the dangerous mission alone to get the milk. Instead, he meets Mahishi and slays her. The gods in happiness and joy assume the form of tigers and accompany back to the palace to give the so-called needed milk remedy. Upon seeing this, the queen confessed her schemes and begs forgiveness from the young prince. Ayappa, forgiving his mother, takes upon the right of celibacy and leaves the palace to rFor further information on the pilgrimage to Sabarimala, consult:

hat he dances every evening in order to relieve the sufferings of creatures and entertain the gods and goddesses who gather upon Mt. Kailash. Shiva is believed to have manifested in the Nataraja dancing form at the celebrated pilgrimage shrine of Chidambaram in Tamil Nadu state, also shown on this web site.

Khajuraho

Khajuraho Vishvanath

Vishvanath Temple, Khajuraho

Located in the Indian state of Madhya Pradesh and roughly 620 kilometers (385 miles) southeast of New Delhi, the temples of Khajuraho are famous for their so-called "erotic sculptures". Khajuraho was the cultural capital of the Chandela Rajputs, a Hindu dynasty that ruled from the 10th to 12th centuries. There were originally more than 80 temples, both Hindu and Jain, but only 25 are left standing over an area of approximately 20 square kilometers (8 square miles).

The Khajuraho temples were built with precisely carved sandstone blocks, weighing as much as 20 tones, which were held in place by gravity, not with mortar. Oriented in an East-West direction, with their openings facing east, the temples have three main compartments: an entrance, a vestibule, and an inner sanctuary. In some of the larger temples windows were used to bring light into the sanctuaries.

Both the exteriors and interiors of the temples are adorned with exquisite sculptures depicting various forms of the gods and goddesses, as well as the everyday life of people during the Chandela dynastic period in which the sculptures were made. There are sculptures showing farmers, potters, craftsman, musicians and women applying makeup, as well as elephants hauling large loads.

Khajuraho Sculpture

Khajuraho sculpture

Less than 10% of the sculptures on the Khajuraho temples are of an erotic nature, yet since such images are extremely rare in Hindu temples of the medieval period, they have received an inordinate amount of attention by writers, photographers and tourists during the past two hundred years.

The purpose of the erotic sculptures is unknown. One possible explanation is that the Chandela Kings who built the temples were influenced by the Tantric Yoga tradition, which views the use of sexual activity as a valid means of spiritual practice. A contrasting interpretation is that the presence of a relatively small number of erotic sculptures amongst the much larger number showing gods and goddesses was intended to indicate the emptiness of human desires.

Still another explanation is that the sculptures – both the erotic and the non-erotic - were intended to show the full range of human actions. Whatever the actual explanation, the message of all the sculptures together is enjoyment of the variety of experiences of human life.

Buddhist Pilgrimage in India

Impression of Buddha feet, Bodh Gaya

Impression of Buddha feet, Bodh Gaya

Sometime during the sixth century BC, a solitary, wandering ascetic sat to meditate beneath a shady tree at Bodh Gaya, resolving not to rise until he had attained the ultimate knowledge of spiritual enlightenment. Thus began Buddhism, one of the world's great religions and pilgrimage traditions.

Historians, religious scholars, and various Buddhist sects debate the actual year of the Buddha's birth; it may have been as early as 644 BC or as late as 540 BC. It is, however, relatively certain that he was born Prince Gautama Siddhartha, the son of Suddodhana, king of the Shakya tribe. His birthplace was the forest grove of Lumbini in the hilly regions of what is today northeastern India and Nepal. Miraculous events surrounded his birth. Sages prophesied that he would become either a powerful king or, renouncing his royal life, an enlightened being and religious leader. King Suddhodhana, wanting the former and fearing the later, sought to insulate his son from religious and philosophical concerns by surrounding him with a life of ease and plenty. Enclosed within palace walls, the prince grew to manhood and fatherhood never having seen old age, sickness, poverty or death.

Yet this blindness to the full range of human experience was not to last. One day the prince ventured beyond the castle walls and, witnessing the inevitable sufferings of human existence, recognized the shallowness of his pampered life. Metaphysical questions filled his mind and with them the conviction that he must seek and know the great truth of life. Thus, at the age of twenty-nine, he let go the constraints of family and worldly responsibility to tread the path of self-discovery.

Following the ancient traditions of Hinduism, Siddhartha sought out spiritual teachers, or gurus. Inquiring of their knowledge, he diligently practiced various yogas and meditations. Seven years passed, the last three in extreme asceticism, yet still he had not achieved his goal of enlightenment. Finally recognizing that such practices had served him well but were no longer appropriate, Siddhartha journeyed toward the ancient sacred forests of Uruvela (modern Gaya in Bihar, in north India) with the intention of finally and completely realizing the infinite. Guided by visionary dreams and following in the footsteps of Krakucchanda, Kanakamuni, and Kasyapa, the Buddhas of three previous ages, Siddhartha sat beneath the Bodhi Tree. Touching the earth, thereby calling it to witness the countless lifetimes of virtue that had led him to this place of enlightenment, he entered into a state of deep meditation. Three days and nights passed and his intention was realized. Siddhartha became the Buddha, meaning the 'Enlightened One'.

Buddhist Monks at Bodhi Tree, Bodh Gaya

Buddhist Monks at Bodhi Tree (The site of Buddha's enlightenment)

The Buddha spent the next seven weeks in meditation near the Bodhi Tree. Then, at the request of the god Indra, he began to speak of the great truth he had realized. His first sermon was given at Isipatana (modern Sarnath near Banaras). This first discourse, often called "Setting in Motion of the Wheel of Truth" presented the Four Noble Truths and the Noble Eightfold Path for which Buddhism is so famous.

The Four Noble Truths assert that human beings suffer because of the clinging nature of the mind. There is a way out of this suffering, however, and that is through the meditative practices of the Noble Eightfold Path. Through these practices an individual gains insight into how his or her suffering is caused by identification with the mind's processes. Letting go of such identification, one discovers and increasingly resides in a pre-existing state of inner peace.

The Buddha spent the remainder of his life traveling around northeastern India teaching and establishing monastic communities for both men and women. He died at the age of eighty in the village of Kusinara (modern Kushinager, Uttar Pradesh state, India), and his death is known as the parinirvana, the 'going beyond nirvana'. His body was cremated with great ceremony and the cremation relics were placed in an earthern jar. Soon thereafter the relics were divided into eight portions and these, along with the jar that held them and the embers of the cremation fire, were then distributed among the rulers of eight territories in which the Buddha had traveled and taught. Legends state that ten stupas (Buddhist reliquary shrines) were constructed to house these sacred objects.

Small Stupa, Bodh Gaya

Small Stupa, Bodh Gaya

The origins of the practice of pilgrimage in Buddhism are obscure. Some scholars believe that Buddhist pilgrimage was initially imitative of the practice among Hindus but later became an integral part of the Buddhist tradition, assuming its own distinct features. Buddhists themselves are fond of quoting certain passages from the Mahaparinibbana Sutta in which the Buddha tells his chief disciple, Ananda, that there are four places "...that a devout person should visit and look upon with reverence." These four places are Lumbini, where he was born; Bodh Gaya, where he attained realization; Saranath, where he gave his first teachings; and Kushinager, where he passed away.

While these places are actual geographical locations and the scene of certain events in the Buddha's life, we have no real proof that the Buddha spoke of the practice of pilgrimage. Contrary to popular belief, the Buddha never wrote any of his teachings down. What records we have of his words derive solely from the remembrances of his disciples. Three months after the Paranirvana, five hundred of his chief disciples met in a cave at Rajagraha and by common consensus agreed upon what were to be considered the main teachings of the Buddha. Considerable disagreement arose among them on the finer points of the Buddha's message as is evident from the fact that by the year 100 BC eighteen separate sects had been formed, each with its own interpretation. The teachings were collected together into what came to be known as the Tripitaka, and they were handed down almost wholly by word of mouth till they were finally committed to writing in Ceylon in the first century BC.

Whatever the authenticity of Buddha's injunctions regarding pilgrimage, the four places mentioned above became known as the Caturmahapratiharya, or 'The Four Great Wonders' and monks and pilgrims began visiting them. Other places associated with the Buddha's life soon became pilgrimage sites in the new religion. Primary among them were the four sites of: Rajagraha, where the Buddha tamed a maddened elephant; Sravasti, the site of a momentous event known as the Miracle of the Pairs; Vaisali, where monkeys offered the Buddha a gift of honey; and Samkasya, where the Buddha descended from the heavenly realms after teaching his mother. These eight sites together were known as Astamahapratiharya, or 'The Eight Great Wonders'.

Buddhist monks at Bodh Gaya

Buddhist monks at Bodh Gaya

Additionally, there were the places where the relics of the Buddha's cremation had been enshrined in stupas (the exact locations of these relic sites are unknown today). Following his conversion to Buddhism in the third century BC, the Emperor Ashoka opened seven of the original stupas and collected their relics. The Asokavadana (accounts of Asoka) relate that the emperor divided these ancient relics into 84,000 portions and vowed to erect a stupa for each portion somewhere in his great empire. While it is highly unlikely that this many stupa reliquaries were actually constructed (the number has symbolic rather than actual meaning), Asoka did establish a number of temples and monasteries that became important sites on the Buddhist pilgrimage circuit.

More important than the actual religious structures Ashoka founded was the impetus he gave to the tradition of Buddhist pilgrimage and, through it, to the spread of Buddhism across the vast Asian landmass. The passion of Ashoka's religious fervor coupled with the force of his imperial patronage initiated and sanctioned both a sacred geography and a pilgrimage practice in Buddhist India. These traditions would be perpetuated by sages such as the 5th- and 7th-century monks Fa-hsien and Hsuan-tsang, who were instrumental in introducing Buddhism to China, and the 8th-century Indian Tantric master, Padmasambhava, who definitively established Buddhism in Tibet.

Besides the funeral relics enshrined by Ashoka in his stupas, other relics of the Buddha such as shavings from his head and clippings from his fingernails began to "appear" or be "discovered" over the centuries. The authenticity of these relics supposedly deriving from the time of the living Buddha is questionable. Just as false relics were manufactured by unscrupulous Christians during the European medieval ages, so also did the practice occur in the Buddhist world.

Many other places became pilgrimage centers as the religion of Buddhism slowly extended its influence across the vast regions of Asia. In general, there were three primary categories of Buddhist sacred sites that arose in the centuries following Buddha's paranirvana. There is no relative ranking of the sanctity of these three types (or of the individual places within the types) nor did one category arise before the others. One category concerns those places that were considered sacred prior to the arrival of Buddhism and were later incorporated into the fabric of Buddhist sacred geography. Such places could have been the shrines or holy mountains of various shamanistic or proto-religious cults, or the hermitages of sages, yogis, and ascetics. Buddhism from its very inception tended to be a proselytizing religion. Its early proponents and missionaries, intent on gaining converts, naturally sought out those places and communities where spirituality had already manifested. This was especially true in Tibet, where numerous Bon-Po sacred sites were taken over by the Buddhists, and in China, where particular Taoist sacred mountains became the abodes of Buddhist bodhisattvas.

The second category of Buddhist sacred site that arose after the passing away of the Buddha were those places associated with the lives or relics of various sages, saints and teachers in the Buddhist tradition, for example, the well known pilgrimage site of Sanchi in central India. The Buddha never visited this place, yet relics of two of his chief disciples, Sariputra and Maudgalyayana, are enshrined within the great stupa.

A third type of Buddhist pilgrimage sites are those that have their genesis in the manifestation or apparition of various deities. This type of site, seldom encountered in the older Hinayana Buddhist tradition of Sri Lanka and Burma, is quite frequent in the Mahayana tradition as practiced in Tibet, Nepal, China, and Japan.

The Mahabodhi Temple, Bodh Gaya, India

The Mahabodhi Temple, Bodh Gaya, India

Preeminent among all these pilgrimage sites, both old and new, is Bodh Gaya, the place where the Buddha attained enlightenment. As mentioned earlier, this site is traditionally believed to be the place where the Buddhas of the three previous ages had also attained enlightenment. No archaeological remains have been found of any structures dating from the time of the historical Buddha; the earliest temple seems to have been constructed by the Emperor Asoka around 250 BC. This shrine was replaced in the second century AD by the present Mahabodhi temple, which was itself refurbished in AD 450, 1079, and 1157, then partially restored by Sir Alexander Cunningham in the second half of the ninteenth century, and finally fully restored by the Burmese Buddhists in 1882.

The Mahabodhi's square, truncated tower rises 180 feet (54 meters) above the ground. Its two lower stories house shrines that have served through the ages as places of homage, ritual practices, and meditation. Its upper portion is crowned by a stupa containing relics of the Buddha. Inside the temple is an enormous statue of the Buddha said to be more than seventeen hundred years old. In front of the Buddha image is a Shiva Linga said to have been installed by the great Hindu sage Shankaracharaya. The Hindus believe that the Buddha was one of the incarnations of Lord Vishnu; thus the Mahabodhi temple is a pilgrimage shrine for Hindus as well as Buddhists. Hindus have been visiting Bodh Gaya since at least the Buddha's own life time, and from the fifteenth century to the early twentieth the site was managed by a lineage of Shiva priests.

Behind the temple are the two most venerated objects in all the Buddhist world, the Bodhi Tree and, beneath it, the Vajrasana, or seat of the Buddha's meditation. The tree standing today, while not the original, is a descendant of the tree growing in Buddha's time. A cutting of that tree was taken to Sri Lanka in the third century BC, where it still flourishes at the sacred site of Anuradhapura. A sapling from that tree was later brought back to Bodh Gaya, where it is still growing today. The Bodhi Tree was harmed, burned, and cut down various times by fanatical Hindus but, according to legend, each time it miraculously regrew. Around the tree and the temple compound are numerous other places rich in association with the Buddha's enlightenment. The environs of Bodh Gaya have attracted sages, yogis, and meditators since the time of Buddha. Such great spiritual figures as Buddhajnana, Padmasambhava, Vimalamitra, Nagarjuna and Atisha have lived and meditated beneath the Bodhi Tree.

Bodhi Tree, Bodh Gaya

Bodhi Tree

Buddhist Monks at Bodhi Tree (The site of Buddha's enlightenment)

Bodh Gaya, located 100 km (62 mi) south of Patna in the Indian state of Bihar, is the most venerated sacred place in Buddhism. It is the place where Prince Siddhartha Guatama, while meditating beneath the Bodhi Tree, attained enlightenment and became the Buddha.

Traditional accounts say that, in the early years of the 4th century BC, Siddhartha Gautama saw the suffering of the world and wanted to be free from it. As a young man, following the ancient traditions of Hinduism, he sought out spiritual teachers. Inquiring of their knowledge, he diligently practiced various yogas and meditations. Seven years passed, the last three in extreme asceticism, yet still he had not achieved his goal of enlightenment.

Near the Bodhi Tree

Impression of Buddha feet, Bodh Gaya

Siddhartha then journeyed toward the ancient sacred forests of Uruvela (modern Gaya in Bihar, in north India) with the intention of finally and completely realizing the infinite. Guided by visionary dreams and following in the footsteps of the Buddhas of three previous ages, Krakucchanda, Kanakamuni and Kasyapa (who had each attained enlightenment at the site) Siddhartha sat beneath the Bodhi Tree. Touching the earth, thereby calling it to witness the countless lifetimes of virtue that had led him to this place of enlightenment, he resolved not to rise again until enlightenment was attained.

"Here on this seat my body may shrivel up, my skin, my bones, my flesh may dissolve, but my body will not move from this seat until I have attained Enlightenment, so difficult to obtain in the course of great periods of time".

As Siddhartha sat in deep meditation beneath the Bodhi Tree, Mara, the Dark Lord of Death, came to distract him from his endeavor. When the earth shook, confirming the truth of Gautama's words, Mara unleashed his army of demons. In the epic battle that ensued, Siddhartha's wisdom broke through Mara's illusions. The power of his compassion transformed the demons' weapons into flowers and Mara and all his forces fled. Three days and nights passed and Siddhartha's intention was realized. He became the Buddha, meaning the 'Enlightened One'.

The Mahabodhi Temple near the Bodhi Tree

The Mahabodhi Temple, Bodh Gaya, India

The Buddha then spent the next seven weeks at different places in the vicinity meditating and considering his experience. For the first week he continued sitting beneath the Bodhi tree. During the second week he remained standing while staring without interruption at the Bodhi tree. The spot where he stood is marked by the Animeshlocha Stupa, the Unblinking Stupa, which is located in the northeast of the Mahabodhi Temple complex. The Buddha is said to have walked back and forth between the location of the Animeshlocha Stupa and the Bodhi tree. According to legend, lotus flowers sprung up along this route and it is now called Ratnachakarma, or the Jewel Walk.

Following these weeks of intensive meditation, at the request of the god Indra, the Buddha began to speak of the great truths he had realized. His first sermon was given at Isipatana (modern Sarnath near Banaras). This first discourse, often called "Setting in Motion of the Wheel of Truth" presented the Four Noble Truths and the Noble Eightfold Path for which Buddhism is so famous. During the remaining 45 years of his life, the Buddha is said to have traveled in the Gangetic Plain, in what is now Uttar Pradesh, Bihar and southern Nepal, teaching a diverse range of people from nobles to poor farmers.

In approximately 250 BC, about 250 years after the Buddha attained enlightenment, Emperor Ashoka visited Bodh Gaya and established a monastery and temple there. As part of the temple, he built the Diamond Throne, or Vajrasana, to mark the exact spot of the Buddha's enlightenment. Ashoka's temple was replaced in the second century AD by the present Mahabodhi temple, which was refurbished in AD 450, 1079, and 1157, then partially restored by Sir Alexander Cunningham in the second half of the nineteenth century, and finally fully restored by the Burmese Buddhists in 1882.

Great Buddha of Mihintale, Sri Lanka

According one to legend, Ashoka's wife, Queen Tissarakkha, had the original Bodhi Tree secretly cut down because she became jealous of the time Ashoka spent there. It grew again, however, and a protective wall was built around it. The nun Bhikkhuni Sangamitta, daughter of Ashoka, took a cutting of the tree to Sri Lanka where the Lankan king Devanampiyatissa planted it at the Mahavihara monastery in Anuradhapura, where it still flourishes today.

The original tree at Bodh Gaya was destroyed by King Puspyamitra during his persecution of Buddhism in the 2nd century BC and the tree planted to replace it, probably an offspring, was destroyed by King Sassanka at the beginning of the 7th century AD. The tree that grows at Bodh Gaya today was planted in 1881 by a British archaeologist after the previous one had died of old age a few years before.

The environs of Bodh Gaya have attracted sages, yogis, and meditators since the time of Buddha. Such great spiritual figures as Buddhajnana, Padmasambhava, Vimalamitra, Nagarjuna and Atisha have lived and meditated beneath the Bodhi Tree. In religious iconography, the Bodhi Tree (Ficus religiosa or Sacred Fig) is recognizable by its heart-shaped leaves, which are usually prominently displayed.

The Golden Temple, Amritsar

golden temple

The Golden Temple (Enlarge)

The Golden Temple, located in the city of Amritsar in the state of Punjab,is a place of great beauty and sublime peacefulness. Originally a small lake in the midst of a quiet forest, the site has been a meditation retreat for wandering mendicants and sages since deep antiquity. The Buddha is known to have spent time at this place in contemplation.Two thousand years after Buddha's time, another philosopher-saint came to live and meditate by the peaceful lake. This was Guru Nanak (1469-1539), the founder of the Sikh religion. After the passing away of Guru Nanak, his disciples continued to frequent the site; over the centuries it became the primary sacred shrine of the Sikhs. The lake was enlarged and structurally contained during the leadership of the fourth Sikh Guru (Ram Dass, 1574-1581), and during the leadership of the fifth Guru (Arjan, 1581-1606), the Hari Mandir, or Temple of God was built. From the early 1600s to the mid 1700s the sixth through tenth Sikh Gurus were constantly involved in defending both their religion and their temple against Muslim armies. On numerous occasions the temple was destroyed by the Muslims, and each time was rebuilt more beautifully by the Sikhs. From 1767 onwards, the Sikhs became strong enough militarily to repulse invaders. Peace returned to the Hari Mandir.

golden-temple-entrance

Hari Mandir, Amritsar, India

The temple's architecture draws on both Hindu and Muslim artistic styles yet represents a unique coevolution of the two. During the reign of Maharaja Ranjit Singh (1780-1839), Hari Mandir was richly ornamented with marble sculptures, golden gilding, and large quantities of precious stones. Within the sanctuary, on a jewel-studded platform, lies the Adi Grantha, the sacred scripture of the Sikhs. This scripture is a collection of devotional poems, prayers, and hymns composed by the ten Sikh gurus and various Muslim and Hindu saints. Beginning early in the morning and lasting until long past sunset, these hymns are chanted to the exquisite accompaniment of flutes, drums, and stringed instruments. Echoing across the serene lake, this enchantingly beautiful music induces a delicate yet powerful state of trance in the pilgrims strolling leisurely around the marble concourse encircling the pool and temple. An underground spring feeds the sacred lake, and throughout the day and night pilgrims immerse themselves in the water, a symbolic cleansing of the soul rather than an actual bathing of the body. Next to the temple complex are enormous pilgrims' dormitories and dining halls where all persons, irrespective of race, religion, or gender, are lodged and fed for free.

Amritsar, the original name of first the ancient lake, then the temple complex, and still later the surrounding city, means "pool of ambrosial nectar." Looking deeply into the origins of this word amrit, we find that it indicates a drink of the gods, a rare and magical substance that catalyzes euphoric states of consciousness and spiritual enlightenment. With this word we have a very clear example of the spirit, power, or energetic character of a particular place becoming encoded as an ancient geographical place name. The myth is not just a fairy tale. It reveals itself as a coded metaphor if we have the knowledge to read the code: The waters of Amritsar flowing into the lake of the Hari Mandir were long ago - and remain today - a bringer of peacefulness.

Shravanabelagola (Sravanabelagola)

The Holy Feet of the Sri Gomatheswar statue, Shravanabelagola

The Holy Feet of the Sri Gomatheswar statue, Shravanabelagola (Sravanabelagola)

The hill of Shravanabelagola, 120 kilometers west of Bangalore in the state of Karnataka, is a noted place of pilgrimage for the Jains. The large hill, also called Vindhyagiri or Per-kalbappu, is 3347 feet above sea level. A flight of 614 steps, finely chiseled into the granite of the mountain, leads to the summit, where stands an open court and the great statue of Sri Gomatheswar. Shravanabelagolameans 'the monk on the top of the hill' and hermits, mystics and ascetics have resided here since at least the 3rd century BC. In those early times the hill was thickly wooded and hermits could feed themselves from the vegitation of the forest. Near the middle of the 10th century AD, temples began to be constructed upon the hill and from that time the place has become one of the most important pilgrimage sites of the Jain religion. The 58 foot, 8 inch statue of Sri Gomatheswar, carved between 978-993 AD, out of the granite bedrock of the mountain is the tallest free-standing statue in the world. Sri Gomatheswar, also known as Bahubali, was the son of the legendary first Tirthankara, Adinatha (tirthankaras are the mythical, enlightened sages of Jainism).

The chief festival of Shravanabelagola is called Maha Masthaka Abhisheka, or the 'Head Anointing Ceremony'. Prior to the festival an enormous wooden scaffolding is built around the statue of Sri Gomatheswar and more than one million pilgrims assemble around and upon the slopes of the sacred hill. During the climax of the festival, priests and devotees standing atop the scaffolding chant holy mantras and ritually pour thousands of gallons of milk, honey and precious herbs over the head of the statue. While flowing downwards over the body of the statue these sacred offerings are believed to acquire a powerful charge of spiritual energy from the great deity. Collected at the feet of the statue and distributed to the throngs of waiting pilgrims, the magical libations are considered to assist individuals in their quest for enlightenment. The festival is performed only once every twelve to fourteen years during periods of rare astrological significance. Recent festivals occurred in February 1981, December 1993, and February 2006.

Shatrunajaya

Tirthankara statues at Shatrunajaya

Tirthankara statues at Shatrunajaya

While the majority of pilgrimage places in India are sacred to the followers of Hinduism, there are numerous holy sites of other religions such as Jainism, Buddhism and Islam. Jainism is a religion and philosophy native to India founded in about the 6th century BC by the sage Mahavira. Born in 599 BC near Patna in what is now Bihar state, Mahavira began the life of an ascetic at the age of twenty-eight. After years of hardship and meditation he attained enlightenment and thereafter taught for about thirty years before he died in 527 BC. An elder contemporary of the Buddha, he is referred to in early Buddhist writings as Nataputra.

Jainism, which does not espouse belief in a creator god, has as its ethical core the doctrine of Ahimsa, or non-injury to all living creatures, and as its religious ideal the perfection of human nature, to be achieved predominantly through monastic and ascetic life. Jainism teaches universal tolerance, and its attitude toward other religions is that of non-criticism. It is not competitive and has never cared for the spread of its faith. The Jain people and their temples are deeply peaceful.

According to Jain beliefs, their faith is eternal and has been revealed through the successive ages of the world by twenty-four Tirthankaras. The word Tirthankara is a title given to the (mostly mythical) enlightened sages of Jainism; it means 'ford maker' and indicates a being or deity who has bridged, or forded, the mundane and spiritual worlds and can thereby assist human beings in the same realization. Tirthankaras are similar to the Avatars of Hinduism in that their function is to instruct and inspire humankind while protecting the world from demonic forces. Like the 'tirthas' of the Hindu Avatars (see introduction to Sacred Places of India for more detail on the subject of Hindu tirthas), the Jain Tirthankaras have sanctified specific places on the earth by their birth, great miracles or attainment of enlightenment. The 'tirthas' of Jainism are spread all over India and have been divided into two classes. Those places where the Tirthankaras and other holy persons have attained Nirvana are called 'Siddha-kshetra'; and those which have attained importance because of temples, idols or different miracles are called 'Atisaya-kshetra'. The primary Siddha-kshetras of the Jains are the five sacred mountains of Shatrunajaya in Gujarat, Girnar in Saurashtra, Sametshikhara in eastern Bihar, Mt. Abu in Rajasthan, and Astapada, a mythical mountain of the center of the universe. Other important places of Jain pilgrimage are Parasnath, Champapuri, Pavapuri and Sammeda in Bihar; Sonagiri and the Udaigiri caves in Madhya Pradesh; and Mudabidri in Karnataka.

Shatrunajaya, meaning the 'Place of Victory', is considered the most holy of the Jain sacred mountains because nearly all of the Tirthankaras are believed to have attained nirvana while meditating atop the mountain. Rising nearly 2000 feet above the town of Palitana, the rounded peak is entirely capped with an enormous complex of 863 temples. While some of the temples are as old as the 11th century (the religious use of the site is far older), most date from the early 1500's; Muslim invaders of the 14th and 15th centuries had destroyed the earlier shrines.

Shatrunajaya is considered by many archaeologists and scholars of religious architecture to be amongst the most beautiful temples in the world. Within the ornately fashioned and impeccably maintained temples are found many hundreds of exquisitely sculpted marble statues of the twenty-four Tirthankaras.

These statues are the supreme object of Jain veneration and, while they may be worshipped by some uneducated Jains, they are philosophically intended as objects for inspiration rather than worship. The Tirthankaras, as enlightened beings, are considered superior to mere gods and deities, and thus are viewed as examples for humans, inspiring each person on the long and arduous ascent to spiritual realization. Shatrunajaya is the scene of a great pilgrimage festival on the full moon of each Karttika (October-November). Groups of pilgrims from all over the country flock here, and part of the celebration consists of processions carrying huge pictures of the sacred mountain through the streets of Palitana.

The Temple of Dakshineswar, Calcutta

Kali temple of Dakshineswar

In the year 1847, the wealthy widow Rani Rasmani prepared to make a pilgrimage to the sacred city of Banaras to express her devotions to the Divine Mother. In those days there were no railway lines between Calcutta and Banaras and it was more comfortable for rich persons to make the journey by boat rather than by road. The convoy of Rani Rasmani consisted of twenty-four boats carrying relatives, servants, and supplies. But the night before the pilgrimage began, the Divine Mother, in the form of the goddess Kali, intervened. Appearing to the Rani in a dream, she said, "There is not need to go to Banaras. Install my statue in a beautiful temple on the banks of the Ganges River and arrange for my worship there. Then I shall manifest myself in the image and accept worship at that place." Profoundly affected by the dream, the Rani immediately looked for and purchased land, and promptly began construction of the temple. The large temple complex, built between 1847 and 1855, had as its centerpiece a shrine of the goddess Kali, and there were also temples dedicated to the deities Shiva and Radha-Krishna. A scholarly, elderly sage was chosen as the head priest and the temple was consecrated in 1855. Within the year the priest died and his responsibilities passed to his younger brother, Ramakrishna, who over the next thirty years would bring great fame to the Dakshineswar temple.

Ramakrishna, however, did not serve for long as the temple's head priest. From the first days of his service in the shrine of the goddess Kali, he was filled with a rare form of the love of God known in Hinduism as maha-bhava. Worshipping in front of the statue of Kali, Ramakrishna would be overcome with such ecstatic love for the deity that he would fall to the ground immersed in spiritual trance and lose all consciousness of the external world. These experiences of God-intoxication became so frequent that he was relieved of his duties as temple priest but allowed to continue living within the temple compound. During the next twelve years Ramakrishna would journey ever deeper into this passionate and absolute love of the divine. His practice was to express such intense devotion to particular deities that they would physically manifest to him and then merge into his being. The various forms of god and goddess such as Shiva, Kali, Radha-Krishna, Sita-Rama and Christ appeared to him and his fame as an avatar, or divine incarnation, rapidly spread throughout India. Ramakrishna died in 1886 at the age of fifty yet his life, his intense spiritual practices, and the temple of Kali where many of his ecstatic trances occurred continued to attract pilgrims from all over India and the world. Even though Ramakrishna grew up and lived within the domain of Hinduism, his experience of the divine went far beyond the bounds of that, or any other, religion. Ramakrishna fully realized the infinite and all-inclusive nature of the divine. He was a conduit for divinity into the human world and the presence of that divinity may still be experienced at the Kali temple of Dakshineswar.

Sanchi

Sanchi Stupa

Great Stupa, Sanchi

Sanchi, a small town in the state of Madhya Pradesh, is the location of several Buddhist monuments dating from the third century BC to the twelfth century AD. The foundation of the hilltop temple complex was laid by the Mauryan emperor Ashoka (273-236 BC) when he built a total of eight stupas, one of which became known as the Great Stupa. The present Great Stupa (120 feet/37 meters wide and 54 feet/17 meters tall) is, however, not the original one. It encases an earlier stupa of about half its current dimensions that was built of large burnt bricks and mud.

This Ashokan Great Stupa was vandalized sometime in the second century BC, but was repaired and expanded during the later period of the Sunga Empire (85 BC–75 BC). At that time, the dome was flattened near the top and crowned by three superimposed parasols within a square railing. The dome was set on a high circular drum meant for circumambulation, which could be accessed via a double staircase. In addition to their renovation of the Great Stupa, the Sungas constructed the Second and Third stupas, as well as other religious buildings.

Sanchi Stupa

Great Stupa, Sanchi

Encircling the Great Stupa is a railing, with four exquisitely carved gateways, or toranas, each facing one of the four cardinal directions. It is believed that these gateways were carved during the Satavahana period sometime around 100 AD. These four gateways are the finest works of art at Sanchi and are among the finest examples of Buddhist art in India. They show scenes from the life of the Buddha and his previous incarnations as Bodhisattvas described in the Jataka tales. These scenes are integrated with everyday events that would be familiar to the onlookers and so make it easier for them to understand the Buddhist creed as relevant to their lives. On the stone carvings the Buddha was never depicted as a human figure. Instead the artists chose to represent him by certain attributes, such as the horse on which he left his father's home, his footprints, or a canopy under the Bodhi Tree where he attained enlightenment. The human body was thought to be too confining for the Buddha.

Additional stupas and other Buddhist and Hindu religious structures were added over the following centuries until the 12th century CE. With the decline of

Buddhism in India, the monuments of Sanchi went out of use, fell into a state of disrepair and were eventually completely forgotten. A British officer, General Taylor, discovered the site of Sanchi in the year 1818. Amateur archaeologists and treasure hunters ravaged the site until 1881, when proper restoration work was initiated. Between 1912 and 1919 the structures were restored to their present condition under the supervision of Sir John Marshall, and an archaeological museum was established. Today, around fifty monuments remain on the hill of Sanchi, including three stupas and several temples. Altogether, these monuments allow for the study of the genesis, efflorescence and decay of Buddhist art and architecture for a period of about thirteen hundred years, covering almost the whole range of Indian Buddhism. The monuments have been listed among the UNESCO World Heritage Sites since 1989.

Sanchi Stupa

Great Stupa, Sanchi

Contrary to popular belief, the Great Stupa at Sanchi does not actually contain any relics of the Buddha, nor was Sanchi hallowed by any incident in the Buddha's life. Hiuen Tsang, a Chinese pilgrim who toured India about 630 CE and meticulously recorded the details connected with Buddhist monuments, is silent about Sanchi. Stupa 3, however, a smaller stupa near the Great Stupa, did contain the relics of two of the foremost disciples of the Buddha, Sarriputa and Mahamogallena. These relics were found by Colonel Cunningham in 1851, carried to England in 1853 and finally returned to Sanchi in 1953.

What then is the purpose and meaning of the Great Stupa at Sanchi? A stupa is not a building in any traditional sense. Initially a burial or reliquary mound, it became a symbolic object, a symbol of the Buddha, a symbol of his final release from the cycle of birth and rebirth – the Parinirvana or the "Final Dying" to the world.

In a larger sense the stupa is also a cosmic symbol. Its hemispherical shape represents the world egg. Stupas commonly rest on a square pedestal and are carefully aligned with the four cardinal points of the compass. This is a recurrence of the symbolism of the dome whereby Earth supports Heaven and Heaven covers Earth. The axis of the world is always represented in the stupa, rising above its summit. A ritual circumambulatory path around the monument completes the cosmic symbolism.

Amarnath Cave

Amarnath

Sacred cave of Shiva, Amarnath, Kashmir

The Amarnath caves, located in the Indian states of Jammu and Kashmir, are one of the most famous shrines in Hinduism. Dedicated to the god Shiva, the shrine is claimed to be over 5,000 years old and forms an important part of ancient Hindu mythology.

Inside the main Amarnath cave is an ice stalagmite resembling the Shiva Linga, which waxes during May to August and gradually wanes thereafter. This lingam is said to grow and shrink with the phases of the moon, reaching its height during the summer festival. According to Hindu mythology, this is the cave where Shiva explained the secret of life and eternity to his divine consort Parvati. There are two other ice formations representing Parvati and Shiva's son, Ganesha.

The cave is situated at an altitude of 3,888 m (12,760 ft), about 141 km (88 mi) from Srinagar, the capital of Jammu and Kashmir.

It is a popular pilgrimage destination for Hindus - about 400,000 people visit during the 45-day season around the festival of Shravani Mela in July-August, coinciding with the Hindu holy month of Shravan.

Devotees generally take the 42 km (26 mi) pilgrimage on foot from the town of Pahalgam, about 96 km (60 mi) from Srinagar, and cover the journey in four to five days. There are two alternate routes to the temple: the longer and more traditional path from Srinagar, and the shorter route from the town of Baltal. Some devotees, particularly the elderly, also ride on horses to make the journey.

During the past fifty years, the ice Shivlingam has shrunk in size. While weather does affect its shape and size, many environmentalists blame global warming for the condition.

Sadhus of India

Each year millions of men and women go on pilgrimage in India. Most take a short break from their daily lives and return home upon the completion of their pilgrimage. Others spend years visiting sacred sites all across the country. Notable among these long-time pilgrims are the sadhus. The Sanskrit term sadhu (pronounced sah-doo) refers to individuals who have chosen to live their lives apart from or on the edges of society in order to focus on their own spiritual practice. Members of different semi-monastic orders, sadhus are renunciates who have left behind all material and sexual attachments and live in caves, forests and temples all over India and Nepal. Some sadhus are elder men who have lived as householders and raised families before becoming sadhus, while others are young men who have become renunciates often in their late teens or early 20s (there are also female sadhus called Sadhvis). There are an estimated 4 or 5 million sadhus in India today and they are widely revered for their intense spiritual practices and holiness.

Animistic Shrines of India

Roadside tree-shrine, south India

While India is notable for its great temple complexes, it is important to understand that each of the great temples had their genesis as a small shrine of a rural folk people. Long before pilgrims came to visit from distant lands and long before royal patronage enabled the construction of huge, stylized temple structures, particular river sites, springs, caves, trees and rocks were known by local people to be the dwelling place of a variety of different earth spirits. The first shrines were simple thatch or wooden enclosures built over a sacred spirit stone or beneath a sacred tree. These structures were primarily utilitarian in the sense that they delineated the perimeter of the sacred space and facilitated the gathering of the local folk people for ritual purposes.

The enclosures themselves were not initially considered sacred - they only housed the sacred - yet over the course of time the structures also came to be regarded as sacred. The rock of the sacred enclosure was considered the static, earthly, 'masculine' aspect, the sacred tree was the dynamic, fertilizing, 'feminine' aspect, and together they represented the creative foundation of life. Below the earth of the sacred stone and in the branches of the sacred tree lived the mythic serpent. Winding its way sinuously and easily through the two realms, the mysterious and long-living serpent is understood to represent both realms and, more importantly, to energetically connect the two. Throughout the great expanse of ancient India, from the Dravidian south to the Indus Valley civilizations of the north, the serpent is thus associated with the magical sites of the hermaphroditic earth spirit.